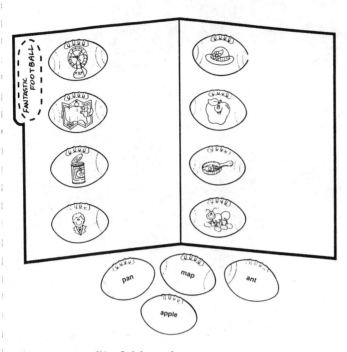

Game: Fantastic Football
Skill: Matching words with pictures
Game Includes: Eight word footballs and eight picture footballs
How to Make:
1. Color and cut out footballs.
2. Mount picture footballs in folder and word footballs on tagboard.
3. Cut out game label and mount on file folder tab.
4. Color, cut out and mount game title on front of folder.
5. Cut out "How to Play" and mount on outside of folder.
6. For durability, laminate folder and game pieces. Store pieces in plastic pocket or bag.

*Mount on file folder tab.

Fantastic Football
Matching words with pictures

How to Play: Match the word footballs to the picture footballs in the folder.

*Color and cut out game title. Mount on front of folder.

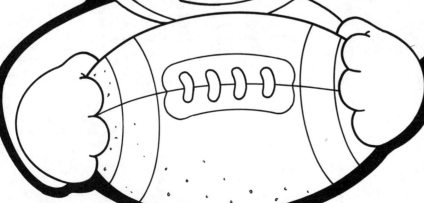

*Color and cut out picture footballs and mount in folder.

Fantastic Football

*Color and cut out picture and word footballs. Mount picture footballs in folder and word footballs on tagboard. Laminate and store word footballs in plastic pocket or bag.

Fantastic Football

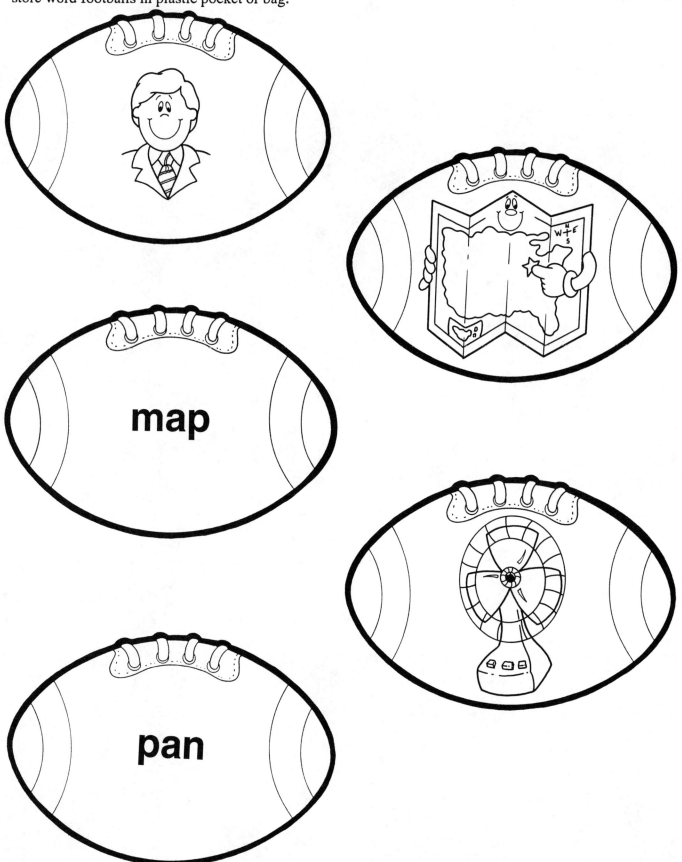

map

pan

*Color and cut out word footballs and mount on tagboard.
Laminate and store footballs in plastic pocket or bag.

Fantastic Football

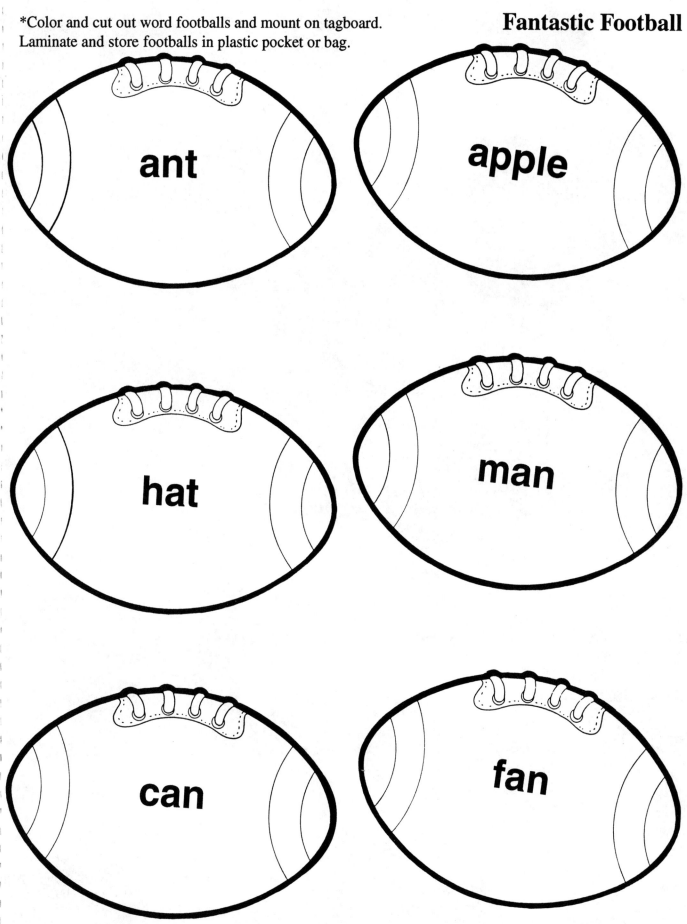

ant

apple

hat

man

can

fan

*Mount on file folder tab.

```
┌────────────────────────────────┐
│          Pencil Perfect         │
│     Matching numbers with sets  │
└────────────────────────────────┘
```

Game: Pencil Perfect
Skill: Matching numbers with sets
Game Includes: Eight pencils and eight erasers
How to Make:
1. Color and cut out erasers and pencils.
2. Mount pencils in folder and erasers on tagboard.
3. Cut out game label and mount on file folder tab.
4. Color, cut out and mount game title on front of folder.
5. Cut out "How to Play" and mount on outside of folder.
6. For durability, laminate folder and game pieces. Store pieces in plastic pocket or bag.

How to Play: Match numbers with sets.

*Color and cut out game title. Mount on front of folder.

*Color and cut out pencils and mount in folder.

Pencil Perfect

11

*Color and cut out pencils and mount in folder.

Pencil Perfect

*Color and cut out erasers and mount on tagboard.
Laminate and store erasers in plastic pocket or bag.

Pencil Perfect

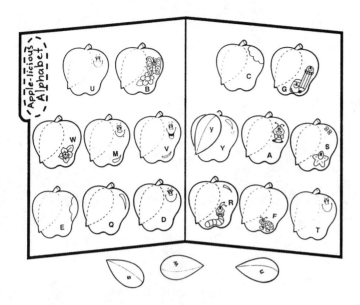

*Mount on file folder tab.

Apple-licious Alphabet
Matching upper and lower case letters

Game: Apple-licious Alphabet
Skill: Matching upper case and lower case letters
Game Includes: Sixteen apples and sixteen leaves
How to Make:
1. Color and cut out apples and leaves.
2. Mount apples in folder and leaves on tagboard.
3. Cut out game label and mount on file folder tab.
4. Color, cut out and mount game title on front of folder.
5. Cut out "How to Play" and mount on outside of folder.
6. For durability, laminate folder and game pieces. Store pieces in plastic pocket or bag.

How to Play: Match upper and lower case letters.

*Color and cut out game title. Mount on front of folder.

APPLE-LICIOUS ALPHABET

17

*Color and cut out apples and mount in folder.

Apple-licious Alphabet

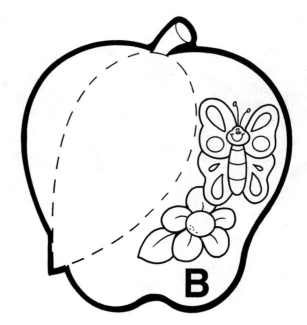

*Color and cut out apples and mount in folder.

Apple-licious Alphabet

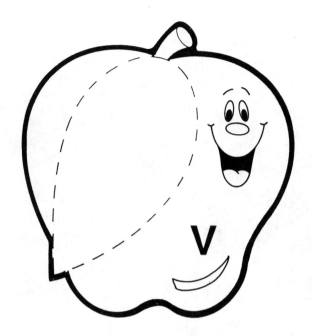

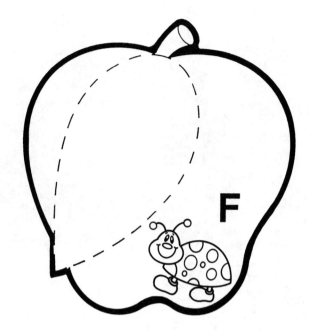

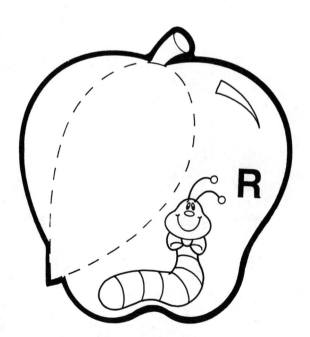

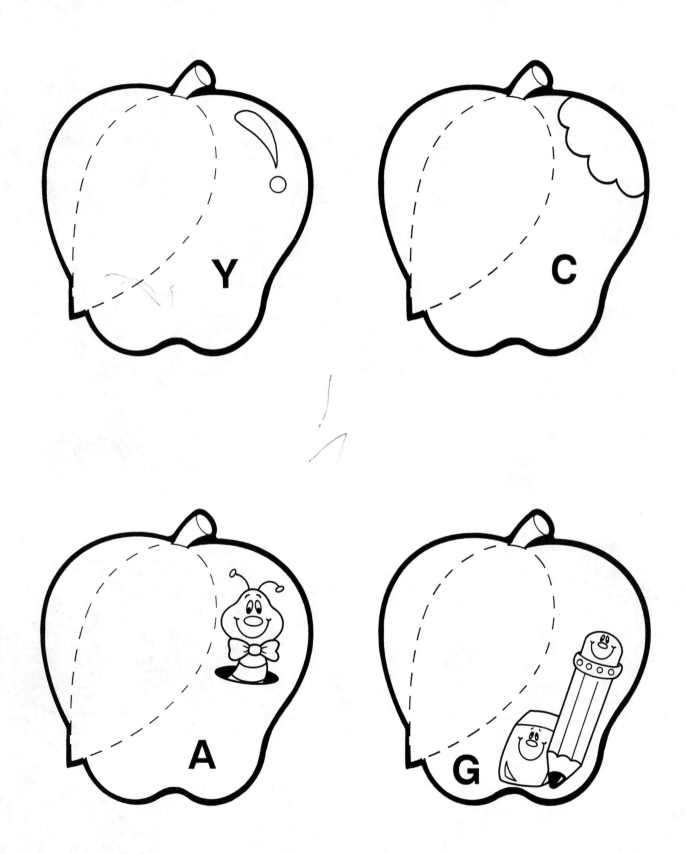

*Color and cut out apples and mount in folder.

Apple-licious Alphabet

E

T

Q

D

*Color and cut out leaves and mount on tagboard.
Laminate and store leaves in plastic pocket or bag.

Apple-licious Alphabet

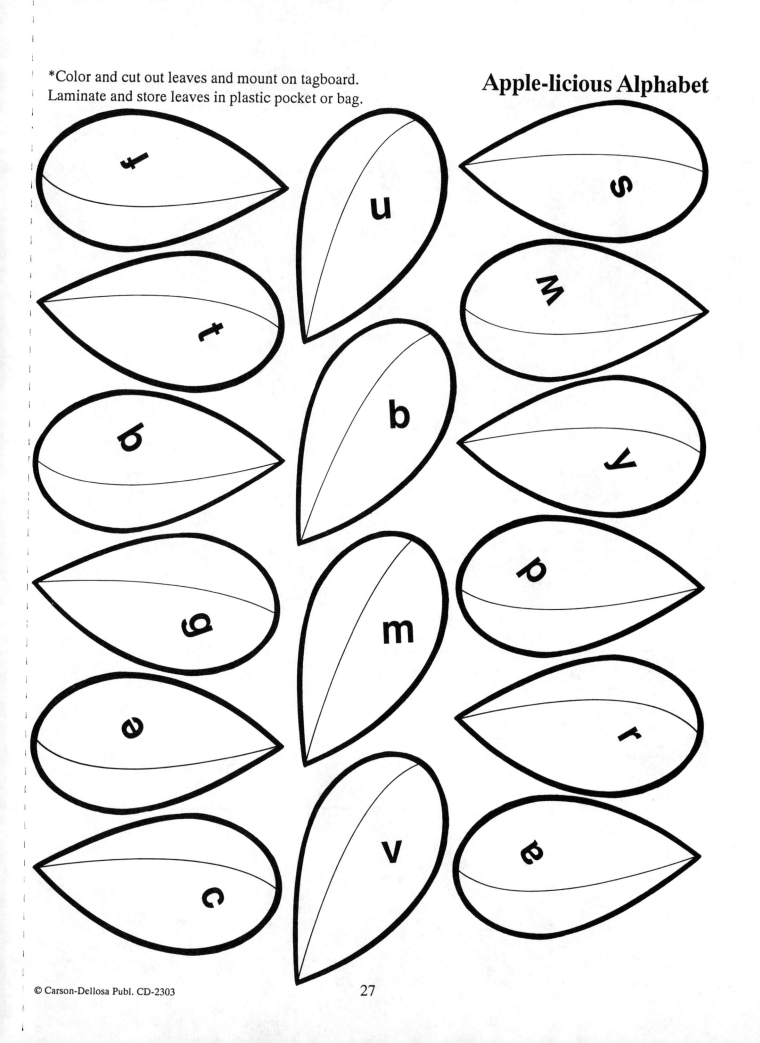

27

Up a Tree
Rhyming words

Game: Up a Tree
Skill: Rhyming words
Game Includes: One tree and eight leaves
How to Make:
1. Color and cut out tree and leaves.
2. Mount tree in folder and leaves on tag-board.
3. Cut out game label and mount on file folder tab.
4. Color, cut out and mount game title on front of folder.
5. Cut out "How to Play" and mount on outside of folder.
6. For durability, laminate folder and game pieces. Store pieces in plastic pocket or bag.

How to Play: Match each picture with a rhyming word.

*Color and cut out game title. Mount on front of folder.

*Color and cut out tree and mount in folder.

*Color and cut out leaves and mount on tagboard.
Laminate and store leaves in plastic pocket or bag.

Up a Tree

*Mount on file folder tab.

> **Spinning Numbers**
> Matching numbers to sets

Game: Spinning Numbers
Skill: Matching numbers and sets
Game Includes: Two webs and eight spiders
How to Make:
1. Color and cut out webs and spiders.
2. Mount webs in folder and spiders on tagboard.
3. Cut out game label and mount on file folder tab.
4. Color, cut out and mount game title on front of folder.
5. Cut out "How to Play" and mount on outside of folder.
6. For durability, laminate folder and game pieces. Store pieces in plastic pocket or bag.

> **How to Play:** Match the set spiders to their web numbers.

*Color and cut out game title. Mount on front of folder.

*Color and cut out web and mount in folder.

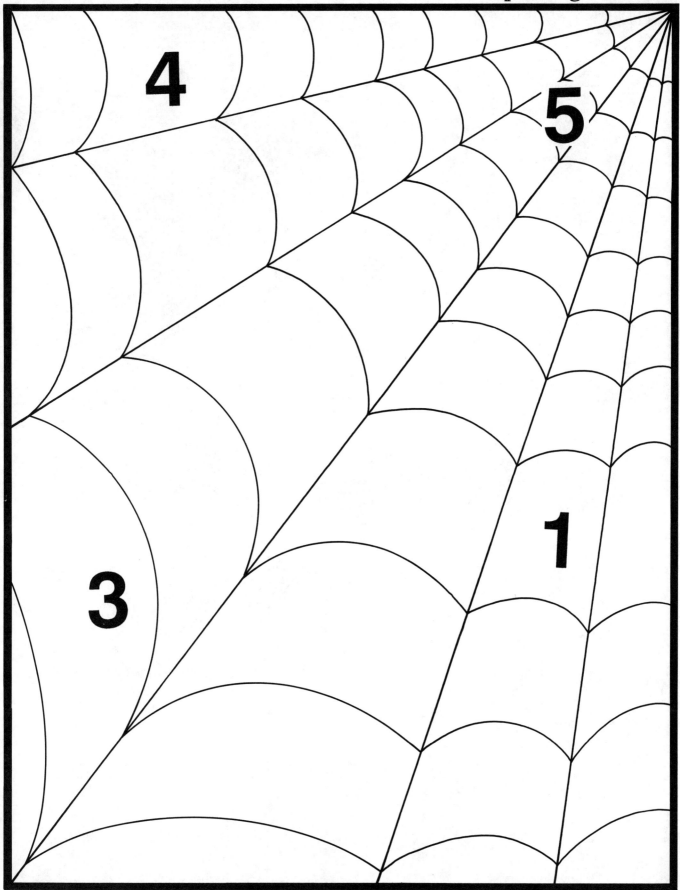

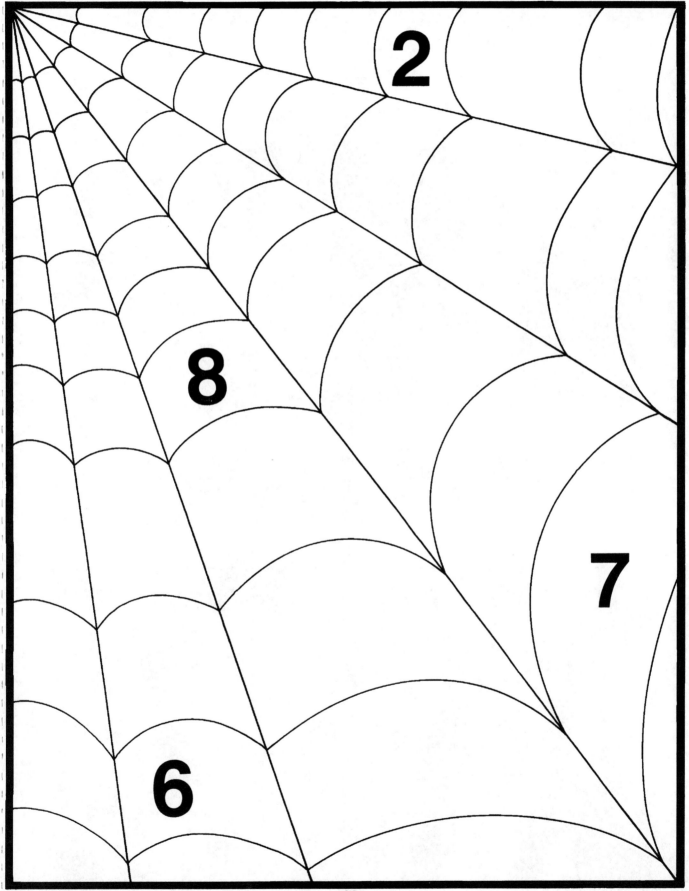

*Color and cut out spiders and mount on tagboard.
Laminate and store spiders in plastic pocket or bag.

Spinning Numbers

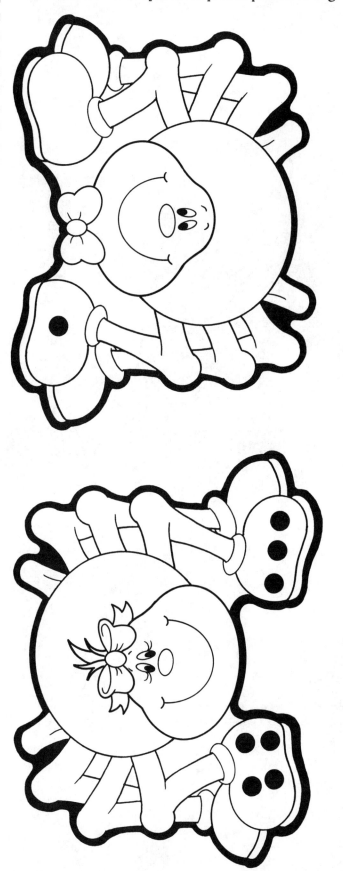

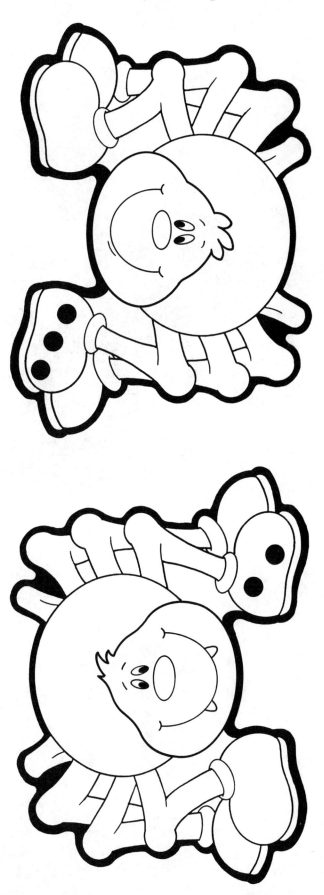

41

*Color and cut out spiders and mount on tagboard.
Laminate and store spiders in plastic pocket or bag.

Spinning Numbers

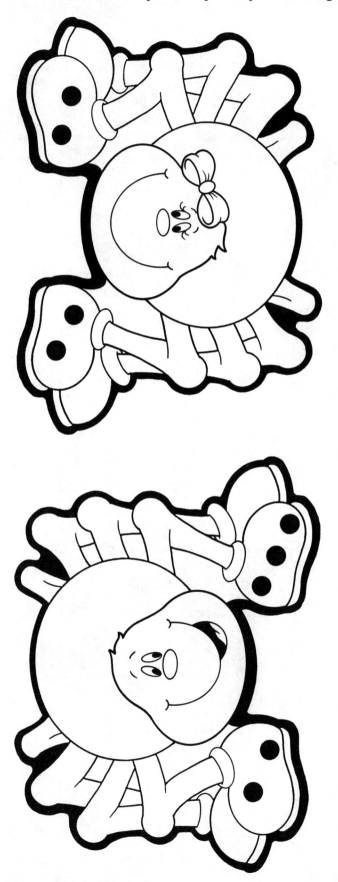

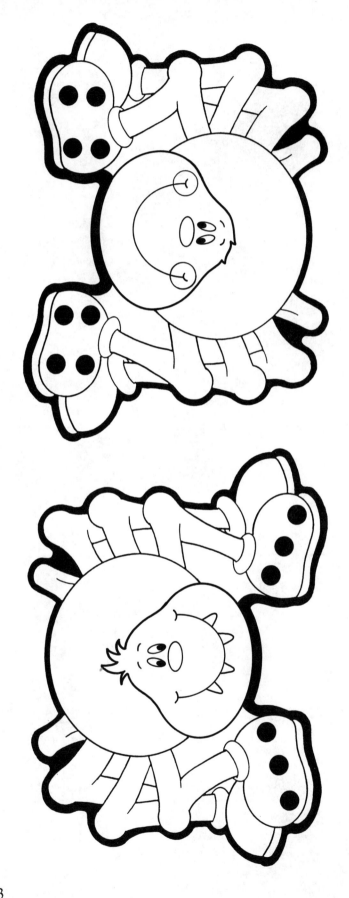

43

*Mount on file folder tab.

Hats Off!
Beginning, middle and ending sounds

Game: Hats Off!
Skill: Identifying beginning, middle and ending sounds
Game Includes: Eight picture frames
How to Make:
1. Color and cut out picture frames and mount in folder.
2. Mount picture frames in folder.
3. Cut out game label and mount on file folder tab.
4. Color, cut out and mount game title on front of folder.
5. Cut out "How to Play" and mount on outside of folder.
6. Cut out "Answer Key" and mount on back of folder.
7. For durability, laminate folder and game pieces. Store pieces in plastic pocket or bag.

How to Play: With grease pencil, mark the beginning, middle or ending box under the picture to show where the letter is heard.

*Color and cut out game title. Mount on front of folder.

45

Answer Key
bat
cat
ghost
spi**d**er
hat
pump**k**in
mo**n**ster
frog

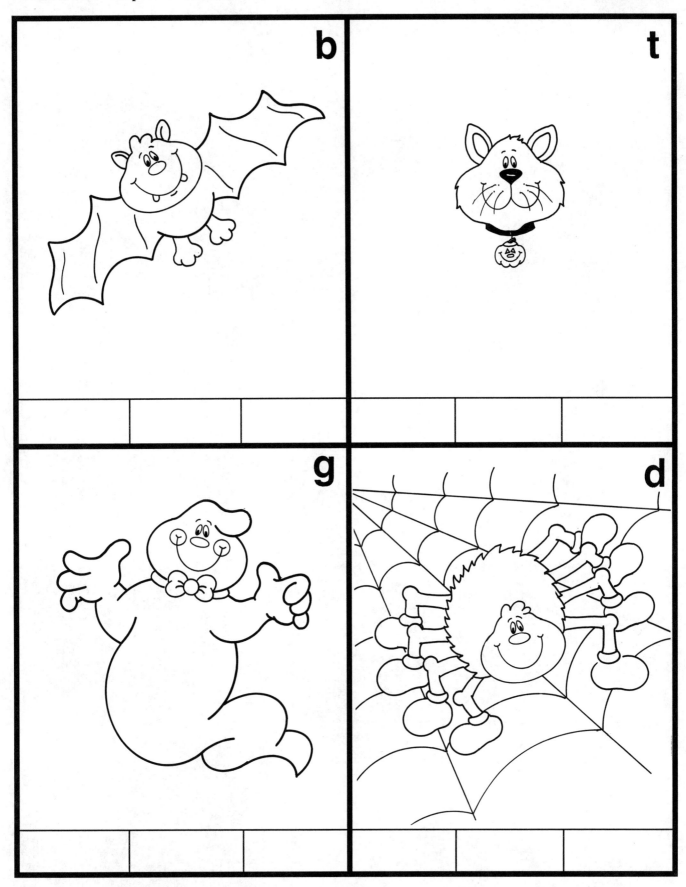

*Color and cut out picture frames and mount in folder.

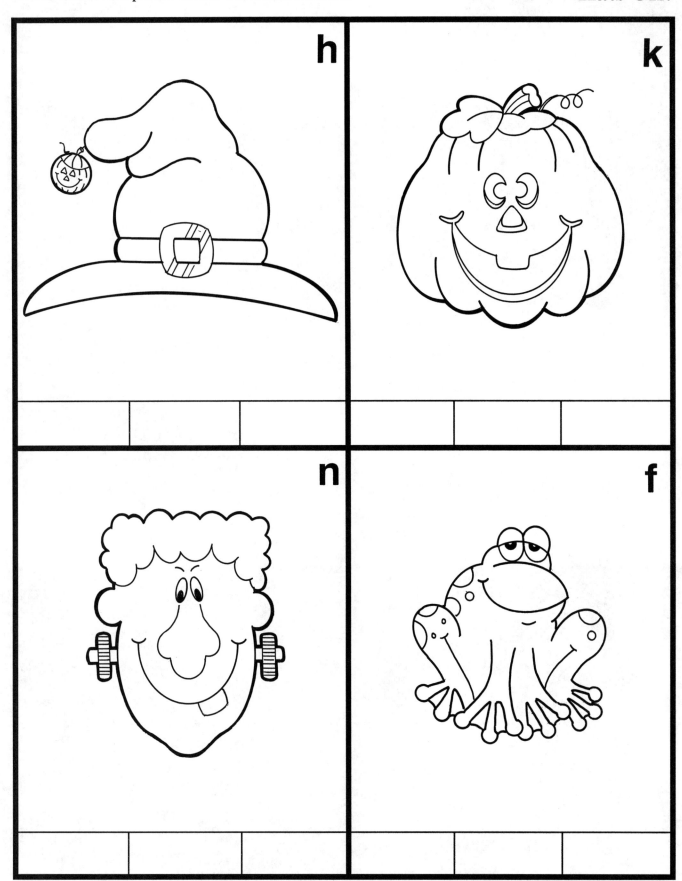

*Mount on file folder tab.

Patch Match
Matching identical pictures

Game: Patch Match
Skill: Matching identical pictures
Game Includes: Two game board pieces and six pumpkins
How to Make:
1. Color and cut out pumpkin game boards and pumpkins.
2. Mount game boards in folder and pumpkins on tagboard.
3. Cut out game label and mount on file folder tab.
4. Color, cut out and mount game title on front of folder.
5. Cut out "How to Play" and mount on outside of folder.
6. For durability, laminate folder and game pieces. Store pieces in plastic pocket or bag.

How to Play: Match the pumpkins that look alike.

*Color and cut out game title. Mount on front of folder.

*Color and cut out game board and mount in folder.

Patch Match

53

*Color and cut out game board and mount in folder.

Patch Match

*Color and cut out pumpkins and mount on tagboard.
Laminate and store pumpkins in plastic pocket or bag.

Patch Match

57

*Mount on file folder tab.

Matching Families
Grouping objects

Game: Matching Families
Skill: Grouping objects
Game Includes: Four game columns and twelve picture cards
How to Make:
1. Color and cut out columns and cards.
2. Mount columns in folder and cards on tagboard.
3. Cut out game label and mount on file folder tab.
4. Color, cut out and mount game title on front of folder.
5. Cut out "How to Play" and mount on outside of folder.
6. For durability, laminate folder and game pieces. Store pieces in plastic pocket or bag.

How to Play: Place cards in correct column to make a family group.

*Color and cut out game title. Mount on front of folder.

*Color and cut out columns and mount in folder.

Matching Families

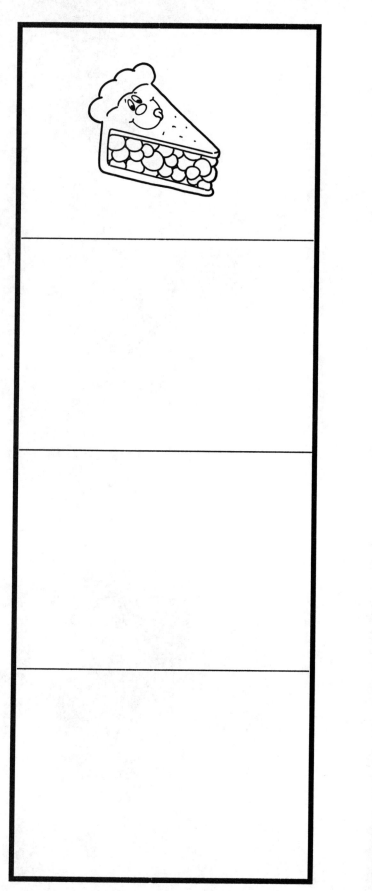

*Color and cut out columns and mount in folder.

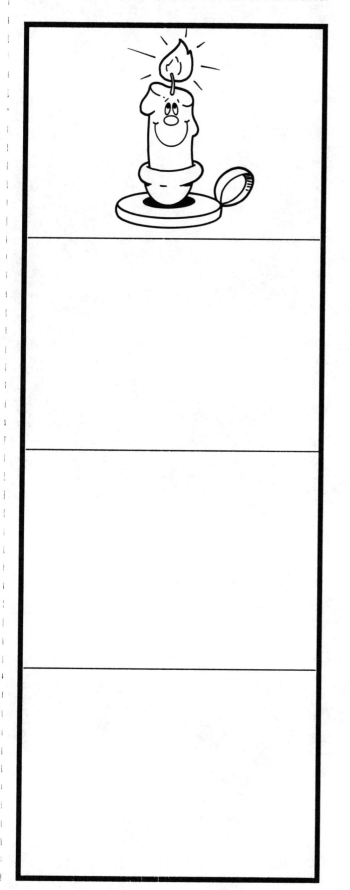

63

*Color and cut out picture cards and mount on tagboard. Laminate and store cards in plastic pocket or bag.

Matching Families

*Color and cut out picture cards and mount on tagboard.
Laminate and store cards in plastic pocket or bag.

Matching Families

*Mount on file folder tab.

Haunted Numbers
Matching numerals to words

Game: Haunted Numbers
Skill: Matching numerals to words
Game Includes: One haunted house and six pumpkins
How to Make:
1. Color and cut out haunted house and pumpkins.
2. Mount haunted house in folder and pumpkins on tagboard.
3. Cut out game label and mount on file folder tab.
4. Color, cut out and mount game title on front of folder.
5. Cut out "How to Play" and mount on outside of folder.
6. For durability, laminate folder and game pieces. Store pieces in plastic pocket or bag.

How to Play: Match each pumpkin to its number on the haunted house.

*Color and cut out game title. Mount on front of folder.

*Color and cut out haunted house and mount in folder.

Haunted Numbers

*Color and cut out pumpkins and mount on tagboard.
Laminate and store pumpkins in plastic pocket or bag.

Haunted Numbers

one

three

five

two

four

six

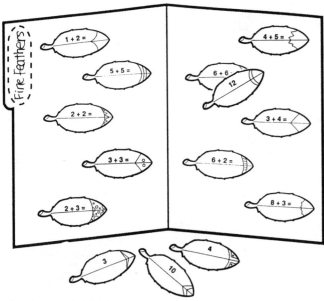

*Mount on file folder tab.

Fine Feathers
Identifying number sequences

Game: Fine Feathers
Skill: Identifying number sequences
Game Includes: Ten equation feathers and ten answer feathers
How to Make:
1. Color and cut out feathers.
2. Mount equation feathers in folder and answer feathers on tagboard.
3. Cut out game label and mount on file folder tab.
4. Color, cut out and mount game title on front of folder.
5. Cut out "How to Play" and mount on outside of folder.
6. For durability, laminate folder and game pieces. Store pieces in plastic pocket or bag.

How to Play: Match the correct feather to solve the problem.

*Color and cut out game title. Mount on front of folder.

Answer Key
$1 + 2 = 3$
$4 + 5 = 9$
$3 + 4 = 7$
$5 + 5 = 10$
$2 + 3 = 5$
$6 + 2 = 8$
$1 + 2 = 3$
$3 + 3 = 6$
$8 + 3 = 11$
$6 + 6 = 12$

*Color and cut out feathers and mount in folder.

Fine Feathers

$1 + 2 =$

$5 + 5 =$

$2 + 2 =$

$6 + 6 =$

$4 + 5 =$

$2 + 3 =$

$3 + 3 =$

*Color and cut out problem and answer feathers. Mount problem feathers in folder and answer feathers on tagboard. Laminate and store answer feathers in plastic pocket or bag.

Fine Feathers

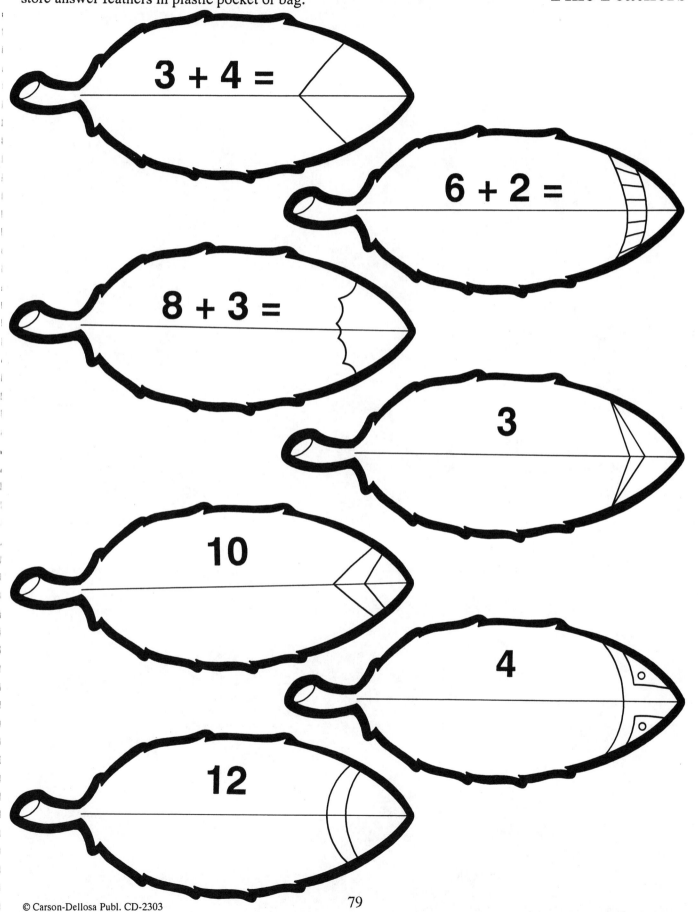

$3 + 4 =$

$6 + 2 =$

$8 + 3 =$

3

10

4

12

*Color and cut out feathers and mount on tagboard.
Laminate and store feathers in plastic pocket or bag.

Fine Feathers

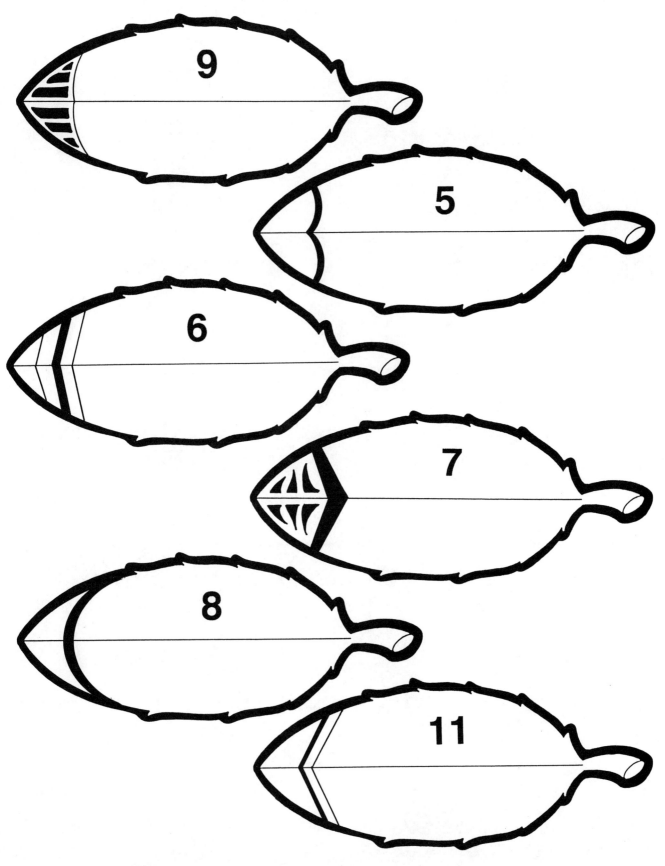

*Mount on file folder tab.

Pickin' Pumpkins
Identifying long and short "i"

Game: Pickin' Pumpkins
Skill: Identifying long and short "i"
Game Includes: Two pumpkins and eight leaves

How to Make:
1. Color and cut out pumpkins and leaves.
2. Mount pumpkins in folder and leaves on tagboard.
3. Cut out game label and mount on file folder tab.
4. Color, cut out and mount game title on front of folder.
5. Cut out "How to Play" and mount on outside of folder.
6. For durability, laminate folder and game pieces. Store pieces in plastic pocket or bag.

How to Play: Match leaves to correct long or short "i" pumpkin.

*Color and cut out game title. Mount on front of folder.

*Color and cut out pumpkin and mount in folder.

Pickin' Pumpkins

*Color and cut out pumpkin and mount in folder.

Pickin' Pumpkins

Pickin' Pumpkins

*Color and cut out leaves and mount on tagboard.
Laminate and store leaves in plastic pocket or bag.

Pickin' Pumpkins

91

*Mount on file folder tab.

November Numbers
Matching number amounts to sets

Game: November Numbers
Skill: Matching number amounts to sets
Game Includes: Eight pumpkins and eight hats
How to Make:
1. Color and cut out pumpkins and hats.
2. Mount pumpkins in folder and hats on tagboard.
3. Cut out game label and mount on file folder tab.
4. Color, cut out and mount game title on front of folder.
5. Cut out "How to Play" and mount on outside of folder.
6. For durability, laminate folder and game pieces. Store pieces in plastic pocket or folder.

How to Play: Match the number hats to the correct pumpkins.

*Color and cut out game title. Mount on front of folder.

*Color and cut out pumpkins and mount in folder.

November Numbers

95

*Color and cut out pumpkins and mount in folder.

November Numbers

*Color and cut out hats and mount on tagboard.
Laminate and store hats in plastic pocket or bag.

November Numbers

*Color and cut out hats and mount on tagboard.
Laminate and store hats in plastic pocket or bag.

November Numbers

*Mount on file folder tab.

Sorting Nuts
Graphing

Game: Sorting Nuts
Skill: Graphing
Game Includes: Two game board pieces
How to Make:
1. Color and cut out game board pieces and mount in folder.
2. Cut out game label and mount on file folder tab.
3. Color, cut out and mount game title on front of folder.
4. Cut out "How to Play" and mount on outside of folder.
5. Laminate folder and game pieces. Store pieces in plastic pocket or bag.

How to Play: Using a grease pencil, color in as many blocks as the amount of nuts shows to make a graph.

*Color and cut out game title. Mount on front of folder.

Sorting Nuts

*Color and cut out game board piece and mount in folder.

Sorting Nuts

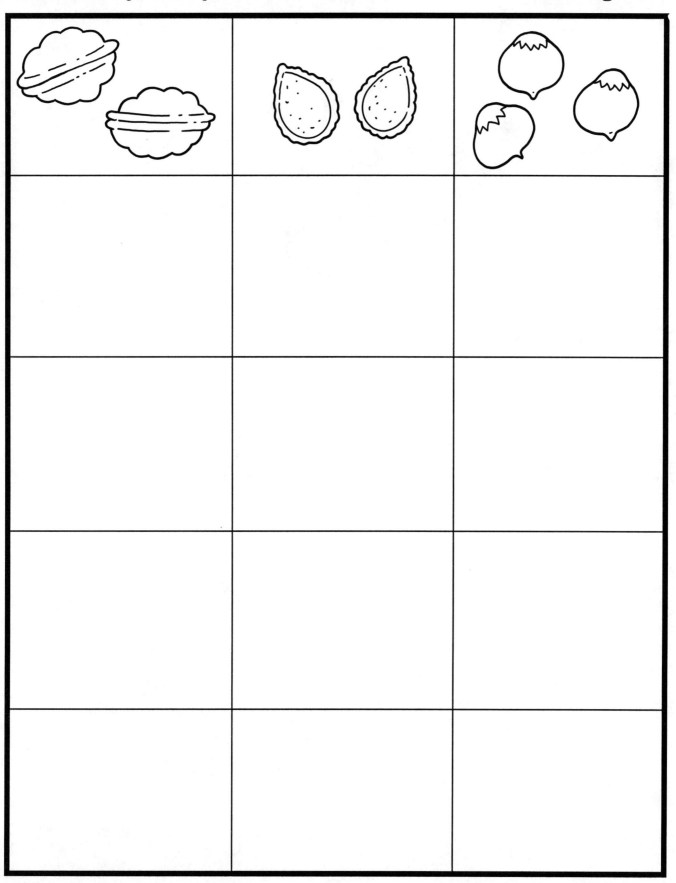

*Mount on file folder tab.

Sweets from Santa
Matching numbers with sets

Game: Sweets from Santa
Skill: Matching number amounts with sets
Game Includes: Eight Santas and eight candy canes

How to Make:
1. Color and cut out Santas and candy canes.
2. Mount Santas in folder and candy canes on tagboard.
3. Cut out game label and mount on file folder tab.
4. Color, cut out and mount game title on front of folder.
5. Cut out "How to Play" and mount on outside of folder.
6. For durability, laminate folder and game pieces. Store pieces in plastic pocket or bag.

How to Play: Match the number candy canes to the correct Santas.

*Color and cut out game title. Mount on front of folder.

*Color and cut out Santas and mount in folder.

111

*Color and cut out candy canes and mount on tagboard.
Laminate and store candy canes in plastic pocket or bag.

Sweets for Santa

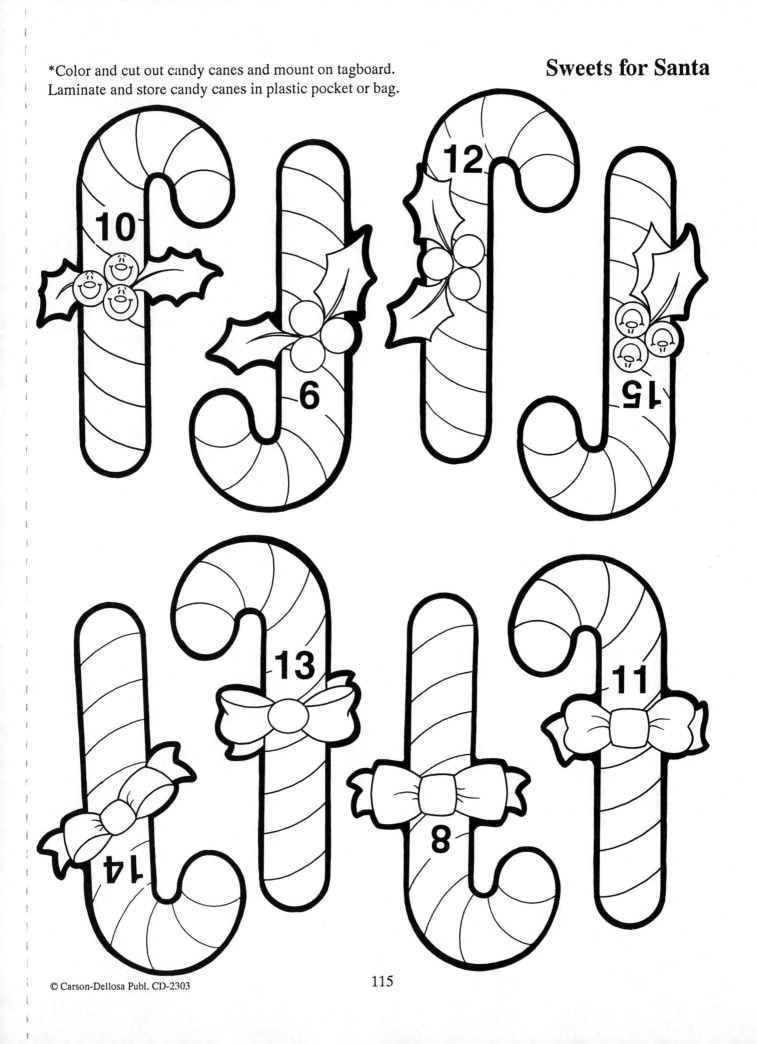

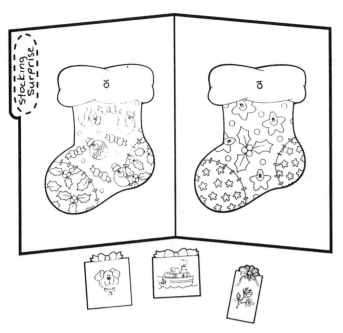

*Mount on file folder tab.

Stocking Surprise
Identifying long and short "o"

Game: Stocking Surprise
Skill: Identifying long and short "o"
Game Includes: Two stockings and eight gifts

How to Make:
1. Color and cut out stockings and gifts.
2. Mount stockings in folder and gifts on tagboard.
3. Cut out game label and mount on file folder tab.
4. Color, cut out and mount game title on front of folder.
5. Cut out "How to Play" and mount on outside of folder.
6. For durability, laminate game pieces. Store pieces in plastic pocket or bag.

How to Play: Match gifts to the correct long or short "o" stocking.

*Color and cut out game title. Mount on front of folder.

*Color and cut out stocking and mount in folder.

Stocking Surprise

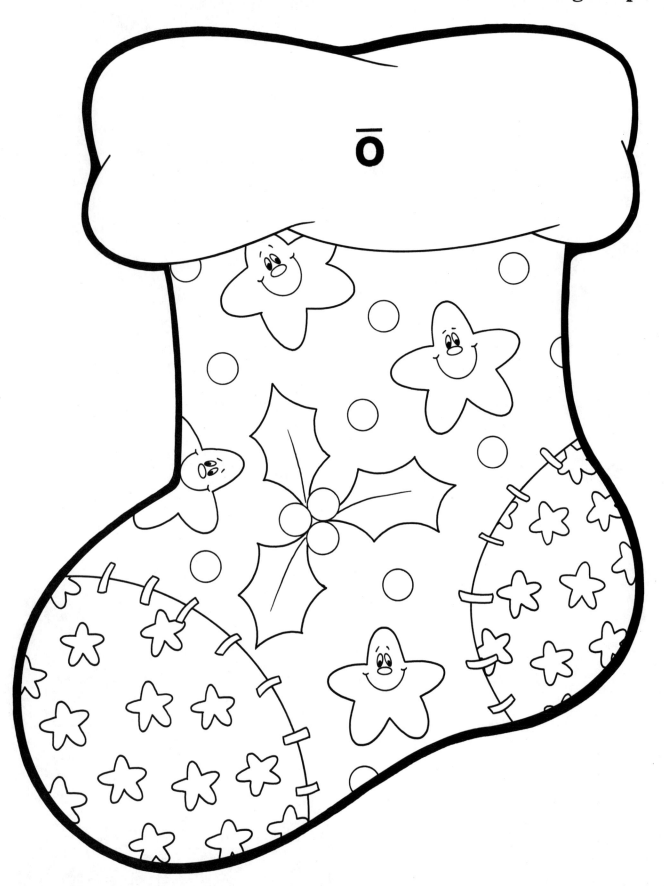

*Color and cut out stocking and mount in folder.

Stocking Surprise

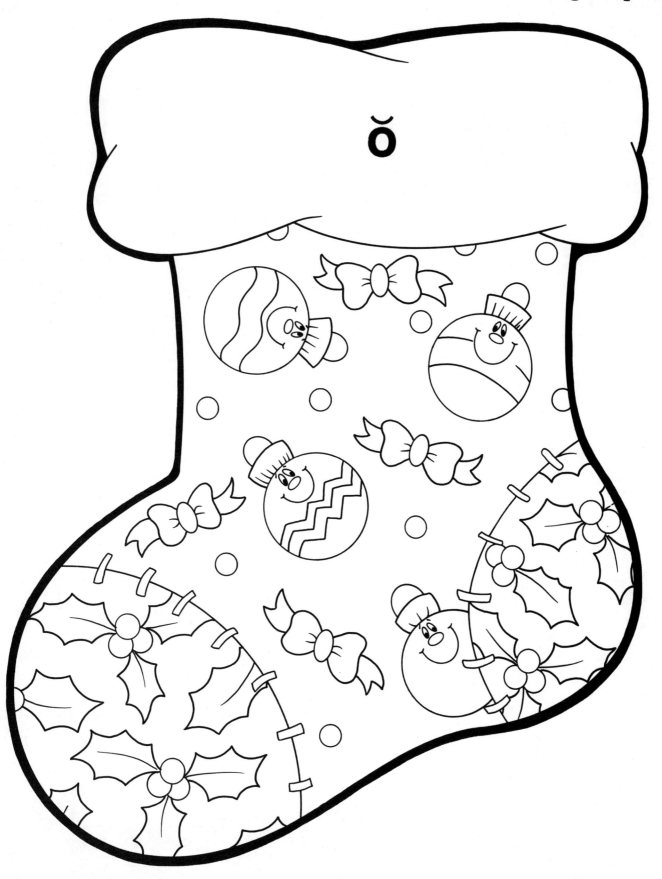

*Color and cut out gifts and mount on tagboard.
Laminate and store gifts in plastic pocket or bag.

Stocking Surprise

*Mount on file folder tab.

Tree Trimmings
Counting pennies

Game: Tree Trimmings
Skill: Counting pennies
Game Includes: Eight ornaments and eight penny ornaments
How to Make:
1. Color and cut out ornaments.
2. Mount ornaments in folder and penny ornaments on tagboard.
3. Cut out game label and mount on file folder tab.
4. Color, cut out and mount game title on front of folder.
5. Cut out "How to Play" and mount on outside of folder.
6. For durability, laminate folder and game pieces. Store pieces in plastic pocket or bag.

How to Play: Match penny ornaments to correct ornaments.

*Color and cut out game title. Mount on front of folder.

*Color and cut out ornaments and mount in folder.

Tree Trimmings

*Color and cut out ornaments and mount in folder.

Tree Trimmings

129

*Color and cut out penny ornaments and mount on tagboard.
Laminate and store ornaments in plastic pocket or bag.

Tree Trimmings

*Color and cut out penny ornaments and mount on tagboard.
Laminate and store ornaments in plastic pocket or bag.

Tree Trimmings

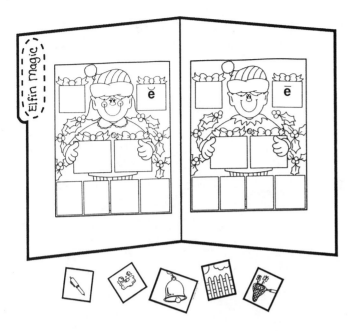

*Mount on file folder tab.

Elfin Magic
Identifying long and short "e"

Game: Elfin Magic
Skill: Identifying long and short "e"
Game Includes: Two elf game boards and sixteen gifts
How to Make:
1. Color and cut out elf game boards and gifts.
2. Mount elf game boards in folder and gifts on tagboard.
3. Cut out game label and mount on file folder tab.
4. Color, cut out and mount game title on front of folder.
5. Cut out "How to Play" and mount on outside of folder.
6. For durability, laminate folder and game pieces. Store pieces in plastic pocket or bag.

How to Play: Match gifts to the correct long or short "e" elf.

*Color and cut out game title. Mount on front of folder.

*Color and cut out elf game board and mount in folder.

Elfin Magic

ē

*Color and cut out elf game board and mount in folder.

Elfin Magic

ĕ

*Color and cut out gifts and mount on tagboard.
Laminate and store gifts in plastic pocket or bag.

Elfin Magic

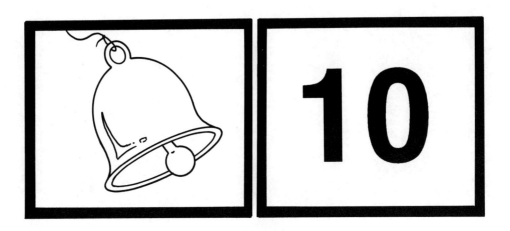

*Color and cut out gifts and mount on tagboard.
Laminate and store gifts in plastic pocket or bag.

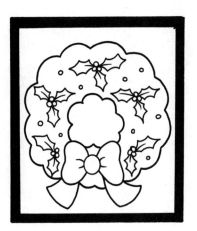

143

*Color and cut out gifts and mount on tagboard.
Laminate and store gifts in plastic pocket or bag.

Elfin Magic

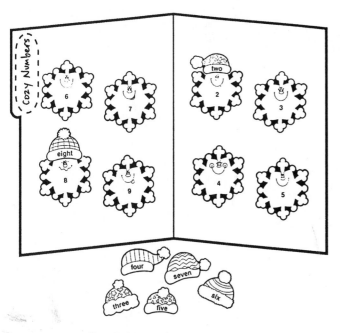

*Mount on file folder tab.

Cozy Numbers
Identifying number words (1-10)

Game: Cozy Numbers
Skill: Identifying number words (1-10)
Game Includes: Eight snowflakes and eight hats
How to Make:

1. Color and cut out snowflakes and hats.
2. Mount snowflakes in folder and hats on tagboard.
3. Cut out game label and mount on file folder tab.
4. Color, cut out and mount game title on front of folder.
5. Cut out "How to Play" and mount on outside of folder.
6. For durability, laminate folder and game pieces. Store pieces in plastic pocket or bag.

How to Play: Match hat to the correct number snowflake.

*Color and cut out game title. Mount on front of folder.

*Color and cut out snowflakes and mount in folder.

Cozy Numbers

*Color and cut out snowflakes and mount in folder.

*Color and cut out hats and mount on tagboard.
Laminate and store hats in plastic pocket or bag.

Cozy Numbers

two

three

four

six

five

seven

eight

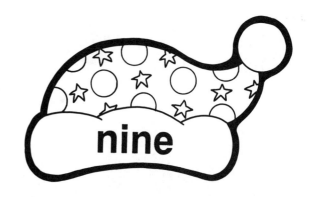
nine

153

*Mount on file folder tab.

Snowman Sequence
Sequencing events

Game: Snowman Sequence
Skill: Sequencing events
Game Includes: Six picture cards
How to Make:
1. Color and cut out picture cards.
2. Mount picture cards on tagboard.
3. Cut out game label and mount on file folder tab.
4. Color, cut out and mount game title on front of folder.
5. Cut out "How to Play" and mount on outside of folder.
6. For durability, laminate folder and game pieces. Store pieces in plastic pocket or bag.

How to Play: Place picture cards in sequence.

*Color and cut out game title. Mount on front of folder.

155

*Color and cut out cards and mount on tagboard.
Laminate and store in plastic pocket or bag.

Snowman Sequence

*Color and cut out cards and mount on tagboard.
Laminate and store cards in plastic pocket or bag.

Snowman Sequence

*Color and cut out cards and mount on tagboard.
Laminate and store cards in plastic pocket or bag.

Snowman Sequence

161

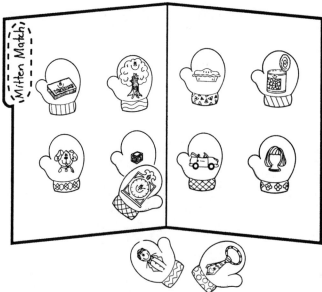

*Mount on file folder tab.

Mitten Match
Rhyming pictures

Game: Mitten Match
Skill: Rhyming pictures
Game Includes: Sixteen mittens
How to Make:
1. Color and cut out mittens.
2. Mount eight, left-thumbed mittens in folder and eight, right-thumbed mittens on tagboard.
3. Cut out game label and mount on file folder tab.
4. Color, cut out and mount game title on front of folder.
5. Cut out "How to Play" and mount on outside of folder.
6. For durability, laminate folder and game pieces. Store pieces in plastic pocket or bag.

How to Play: Match mittens to show rhyming pairs.

*Color and cut out game title. Mount on front of folder.

163

*Color and cut out left-thumbed mittens and mount in folder.

Mitten Match

*Color and cut out left-thumbed mittens and mount in folder.

Mitten Match

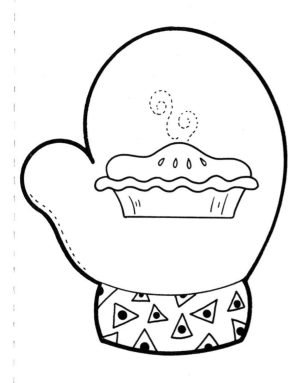

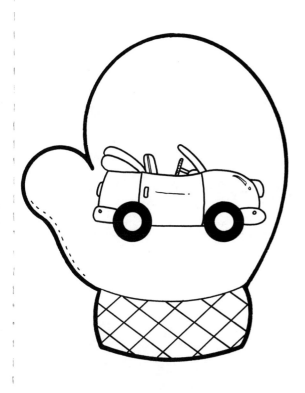

*Color and cut out right-thumbed mittens and mount on tagboard. Laminate and store mittens in plastic pocket or bag.

Mitten Match

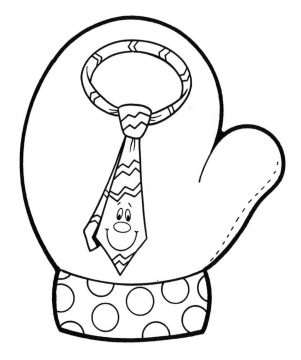

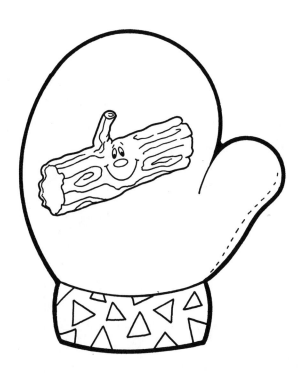

*Color and cut out right-thumbed mittens and mount on tagboard. Laminate and store mittens in plastic pocket or bag.

Mitten Match

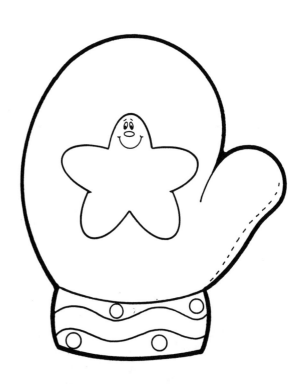

*Mount on file folder tab.

Game: Flighty Addition
Skill: Adding (1-6)
Game Includes: Six birds, two game boards, and answer key
How to Make:
1. Color and cut out birds and game boards.
2. Mount game boards in folder and birds on tagboard.
3. Cut out game label and mount on file folder tab.
4. Color, cut out and mount game title on front of folder.
5. Cut out "How to Play" and mount on outside of folder.
6. Cut out "Answer Key" and mount on back of folder.
7. For durability, laminate folder and game pieces. Store pieces in plastic pocket or bag.

How to Play: Look at bird seed problems and solve by placing the correct bird after each equation.

Answer Key
$2 + 2 = 4$
$1 + 0 = 1$
$3 + 3 = 6$
$2 + 3 = 5$
$1 + 2 = 3$
$1 + 1 = 2$

*Color and cut out game title. Mount on front of folder.

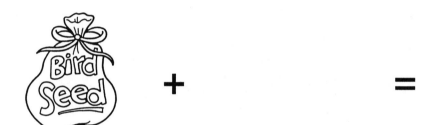

*Color and cut out birds and mount on tagboard. Laminate and store in plastic pocket or bag.

Flighty Addition

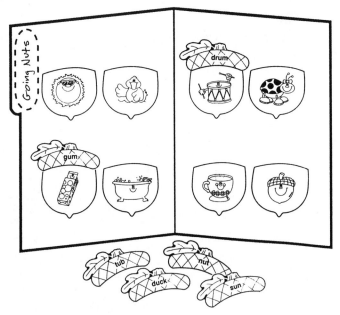

*Mount on file folder tab.

Going Nuts
Matching words and pictures

Game: Going Nuts
Skill: Matching words and pictures
Game Includes: Eight acorns and eight acorn shells

How to Make:
1. Color and cut out acorns and acorn shells.
2. Mount acorns in folder and acorn shells on tagboard.
3. Cut out game label and mount on file folder tab.
4. Color, cut out and mount game title on front of folder.
5. Cut out "How to Play" and mount on outside of folder.
6. For durability, laminate folder and game pieces. Store pieces in plastic pocket or bag.

How to Play: Match words to correct pictures.

*Color and cut out game title. Mount on front of folder.

*Color and cut out acorns and mount in folder.

Going Nuts

*Color and cut out acorns and mount in folder.

Going Nuts

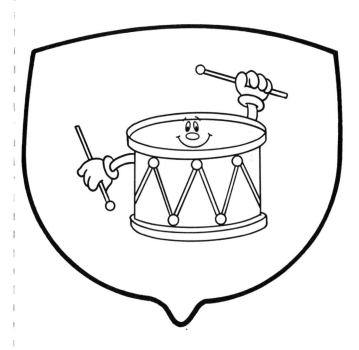

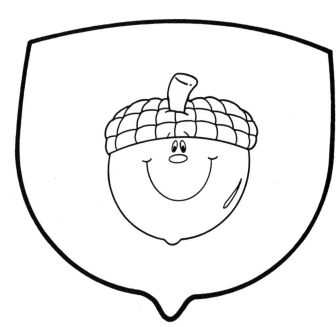

*Color and cut out acorn shells and mount on tagboard. Laminate and store acorn shells in plastic pocket or bag.

Going Nuts

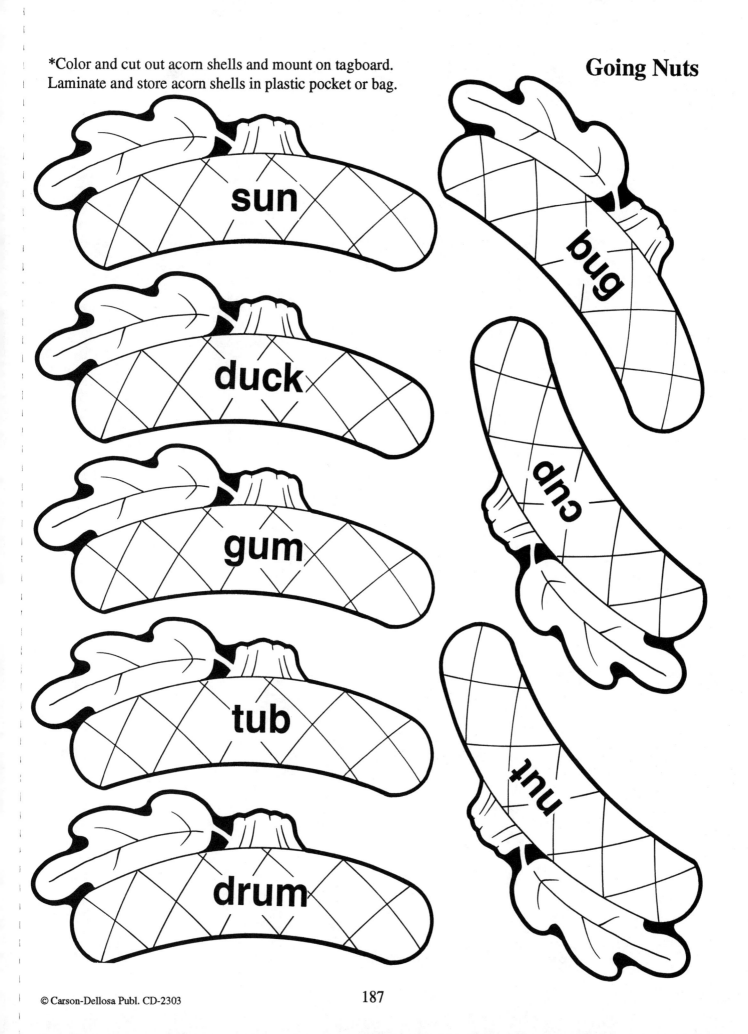

sun

duck

gum

tub

drum

bug

cup

nut

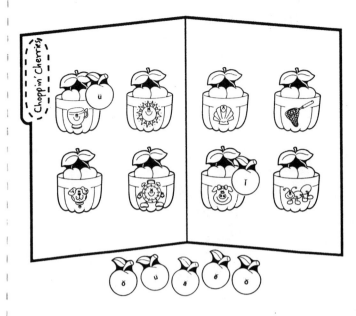

Game: Choppin' Cherries

Game: Choppin' Cherries
Skill: Reviewing short vowels
Game Includes: Eight cherry baskets and eight cherries
How to Make:
1. Color and cut out cherry baskets and cherries.
2. Mount cherry baskets in folder and cherries on tagboard.
3. Cut out game label and mount on file folder tab.
4. Color, cut out and mount game title on front of folder.
5. Cut out "How to Play" and mount on outside of folder.
6. For durability, laminate folder and game pieces. Store pieces in plastic pocket or bag.

*Mount on file folder tab.

Choppin' Cherries
Reviewing short vowels

How to Play: Match each short vowel cherry to the correct picture.

*Color and cut out game title. Mount on front of folder.

CHOPPIN' CHERRIES

*Color and cut out cherry baskets and mount in folder.

Choppin' Cherries

*Color and cut out cherry baskets and mount in folder.

Choppin' Cherries

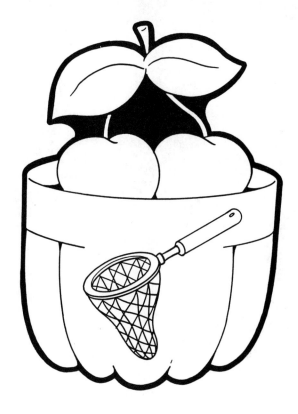

193

*Color and cut out cherries and mount on tagboard. Laminate and store cherries in plastic pocket or bag.

Choppin' Cherries

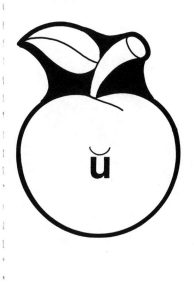

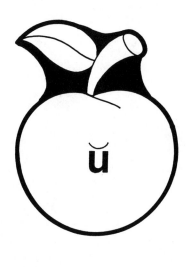

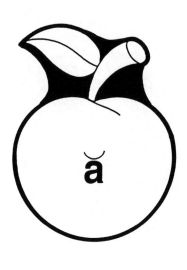

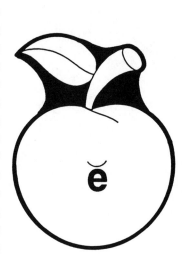

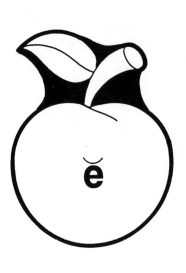

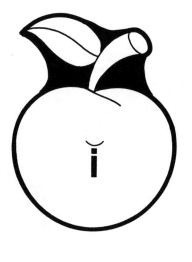

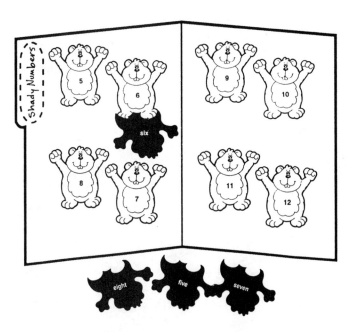

*Mount on file folder tab.

Shady Numbers
Learning number words (1-12)

Game: Shady Numbers
Skill: Learning number words (1-12)
Game Includes: Eight groundhogs and eight shadows
How to Make:
1. Color and cut out groundhogs and shadows.
2. Mount groundhogs in folder and shadows on tagboard.
3. Cut out game label and mount on file folder tab.
4. Color, cut out and mount game title on front of folder.
5. Cut out "How to Play" and mount on outside of folder.
6. For durability, laminate folder and game pieces. Store pieces in plastic pocket or bag.

How to Play: Match each number word shadow to the correct groundhog.

*Color and cut out game title. Mount on front of folder.

*Color and cut out groundhogs and mount in folder.

Shady Numbers

*Color and cut out groundhogs and mount in folder.

Shady Numbers

*Color and cut out shadows and mount on tagboard.
Laminate and store shadows in plastic pocket or bag.

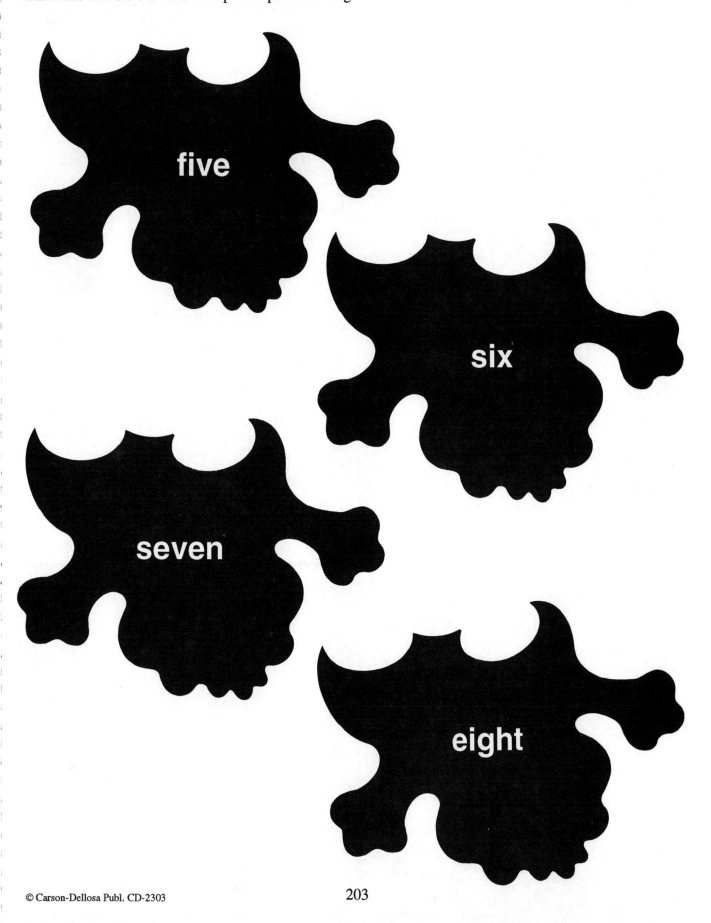

203

*Color and cut out shadows and mount on tagboard.
Laminate and store shadows in plastic pocket or bag.

Shady Numbers

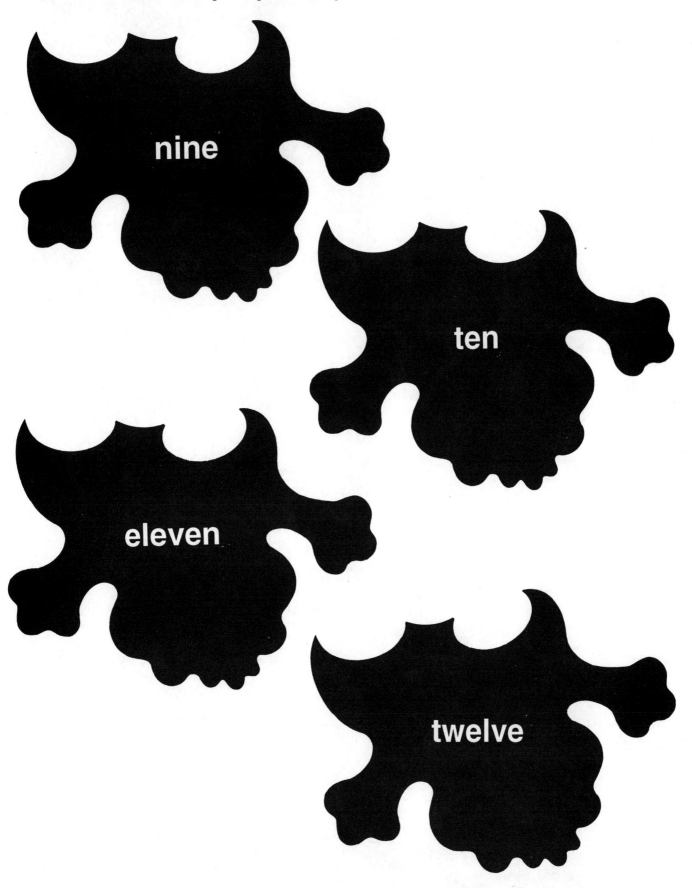

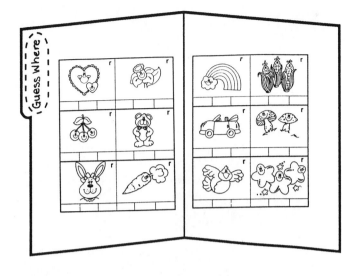

Game: Guess Where
Skill: Identifying beginning, middle and ending "r" sounds
Game Includes: Two game board pieces
How to Make:
1. Color and cut out game board pieces.
2. Mount game board pieces in folder.
3. Cut out game label and mount on file folder tab.
4. Color, cut out and mount game title on front of folder.
5. Cut out "How to Play" and mount on outside of folder.
6. For durability and to make it write-on/ wipe-off, laminate folder.

*Mount on file folder tab.

Guess Where
Beginning, middle and ending "r" sounds

How to Play: Use a grease pencil to mark the box to show a beginning, middle or ending "r" sound.

*Color and cut out game title. Mount on front of folder.

207

*Color and cut out game board and mount in folder.

Guess Where

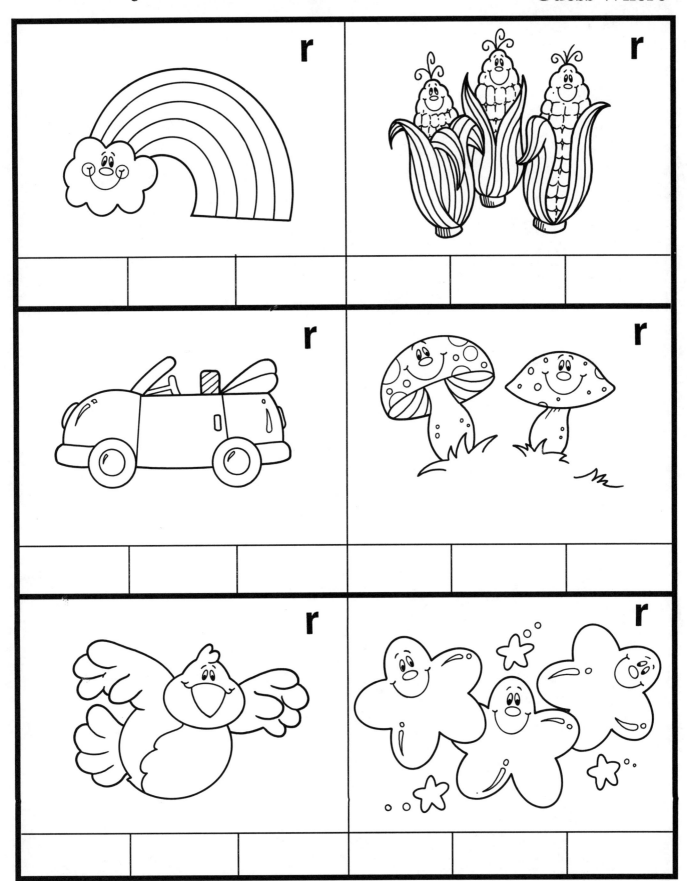

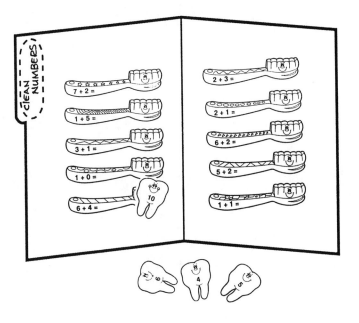

*Mount on file folder tab.

Clean Numbers
Adding (1-10)

Game: Clean Numbers
Skill: Adding (1-10)
Game Includes: Ten teeth, ten toothbrushes and answer key
How to Make:
1. Color and cut out teeth and toothbrushes.
2. Mount toothbrushes in folder and teeth on tagboard.
3. Cut out game label and mount on file folder tab.
4. Color, cut out and mount game title on front of folder.
5. Cut out "How to Play" and mount on outside of folder.
6. Cut out "Answer Key" and mount on back of folder.
7. For durability, laminate folder and game pieces. Store pieces in plastic pocket or bag.

How to Play: Solve problems on toothbrushes by placing teeth with correct answers beside them.

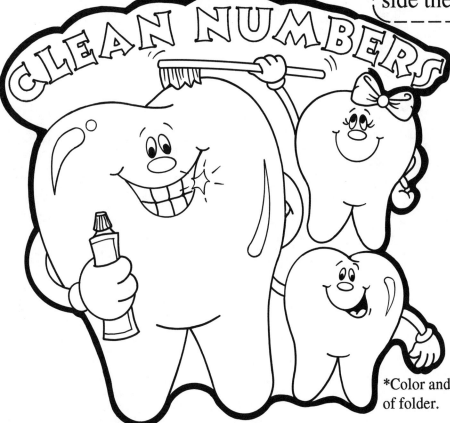

Answer Key

$$7 + 2 = 9$$
$$6 + 4 = 10$$
$$6 + 2 = 8$$
$$1 + 5 = 6$$
$$2 + 3 = 5$$
$$5 + 2 = 7$$
$$3 + 1 = 4$$
$$2 + 1 = 3$$
$$1 + 1 = 2$$
$$1 + 0 = 1$$

*Color and cut out game title. Mount on front of folder.

*Color and cut out toothbrushes and mount in folder.

Clean Numbers

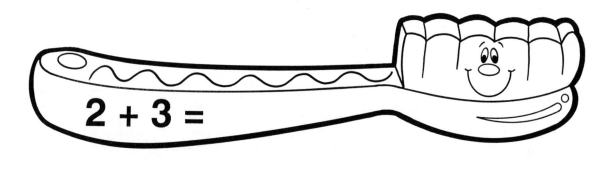

2 + 3 =

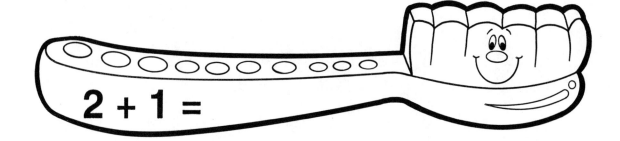

2 + 1 =

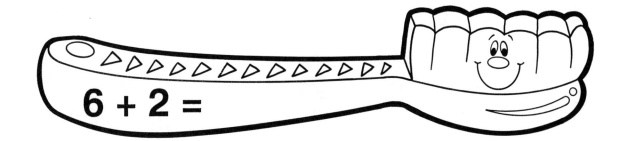

6 + 2 =

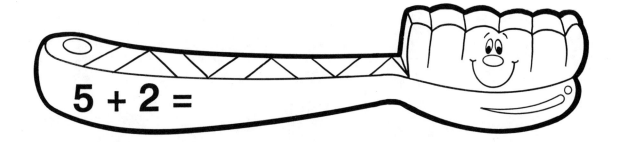

5 + 2 =

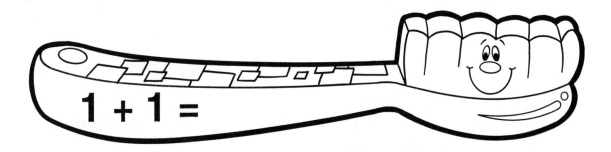

1 + 1 =

*Color and cut out teeth and mount on tagboard.
Laminate and store teeth in plastic pocket or bag.

Clean Numbers

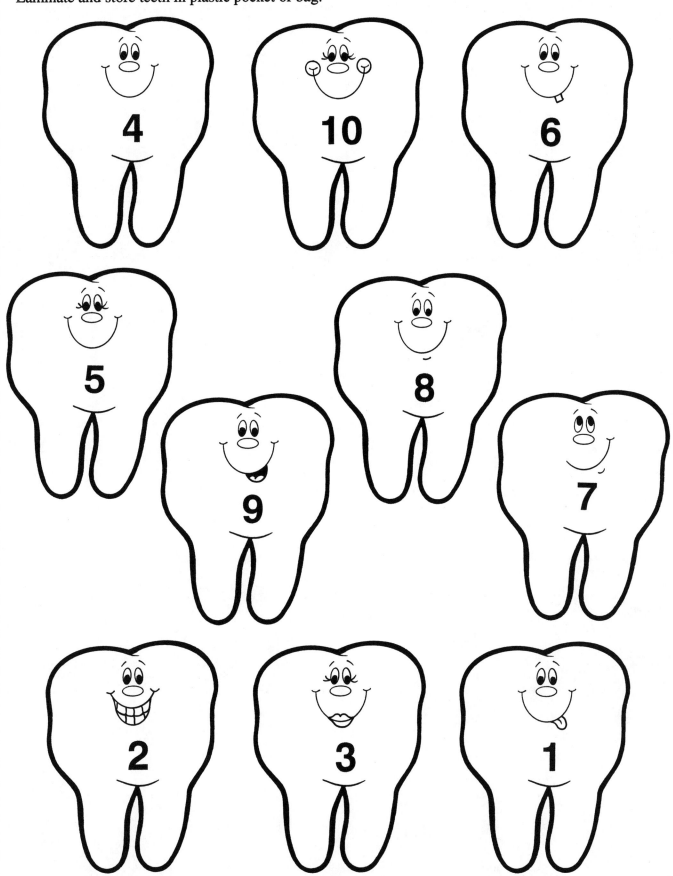

*Mount on file folder tab.

Signs of Spring
Graphing

Game: Signs of Spring
Skill: Graphing
Game Includes: Two game boards
How to Make:
1. Color and cut out game boards.
2. Mount game boards in folder.
3. Cut out game label and mount on file folder tab.
4. Color, cut out and mount game title on front of folder.
5. Cut out "How to Play" and mount on outside of folder.
6. For durability and to make it write-on/wipe-off, laminate folder.

How to Play: Use a grease pencil to fill in the graph blocks to show the number of animals in each picture.

*Color and cut out game title. Mount on front of folder.

*Color and cut out game board and mount in folder.

223

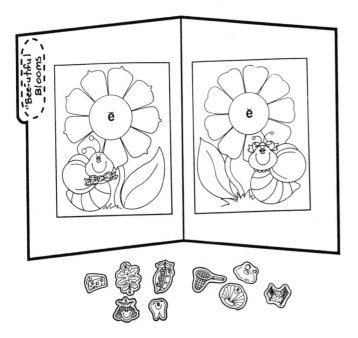

*Mount on file folder tab.

"Bee"utiful Blooms
Identifying long and short "e"

Game: "Bee"utiful Blooms
Skill: Identifying long and short "e"
Game Includes: Two flower boards and twelve petals
How to Make:
1. Color and cut out flower boards and petals.
2. Mount flower boards in folder and petals on tagboard.
3. Cut out game label and mount on file folder tab.
4. Color, cut out and mount game title on front of folder.
5. Cut out "How to Play" and mount on outside of folder.
6. For durability, laminate folder and game pieces. Store pieces in plastic pocket or bag.

How to Play: Place petals around the long or short "e" flower.

*Color and cut out game title. Mount on front of folder.

*Color and cut out flower board and mount in folder.

"Bee"tiful Blooms

229

"Bee"utiful Blooms

*Color and cut out petals and mount on tagboard.
Laminate and store petals in plastic pocket or bag.

"Bee"utiful Blooms

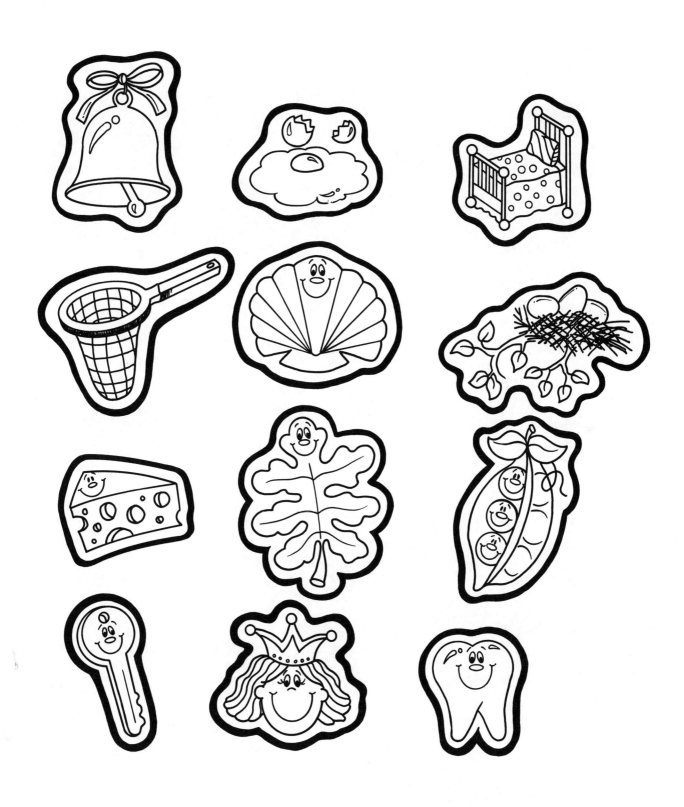

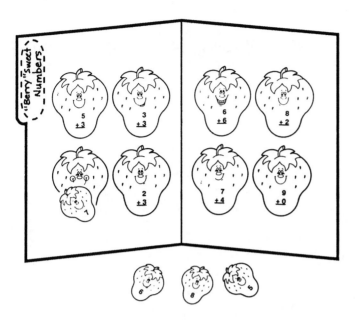

*Mount on file folder tab.

"Berry" Sweet Numbers
Adding (1-12)

Game: "Berry" Sweet Numbers
Skill: Adding (1-12)
Game Includes: Eight big strawberries, eight small strawberries, and answer key
How to Make:

1. Color and cut out strawberries.
2. Mount big strawberries in folder and small strawberries on tagboard.
3. Cut out game label and mount on file folder tab.
4. Color, cut out and mount game title on front of folder.
5. Cut out "How to Play" and mount on front of folder.
6. Cut out "Answer Key" and mount on back of folder.
7. For durability, laminate folder and game pieces. Store pieces in plastic pocket or bag.

How to Play: Solve problem on each big strawberry by placing the correct small strawberry next to it.

*Color and cut out game title. Mount on front of folder.

Answer Key
$$5 + 3 = 8$$
$$3 + 3 = 6$$
$$4 + 3 = 7$$
$$2 + 3 = 5$$
$$6 + 6 = 12$$
$$8 + 2 = 10$$
$$7 + 4 = 11$$
$$9 + 0 = 9$$

*Color and cut out big strawberries and mount in folder.

"Berry" Sweet Numbers

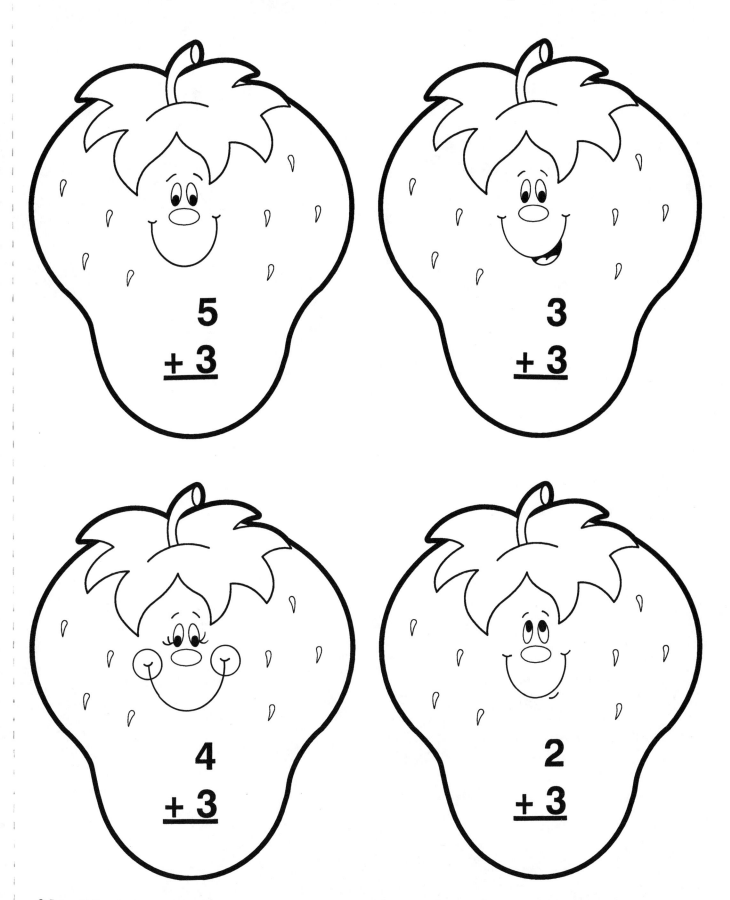

© Carson-Dellosa Publ. CD-2303

237

*Color and cut out big strawberries and mount in folder.

"Berry" Sweet Numbers

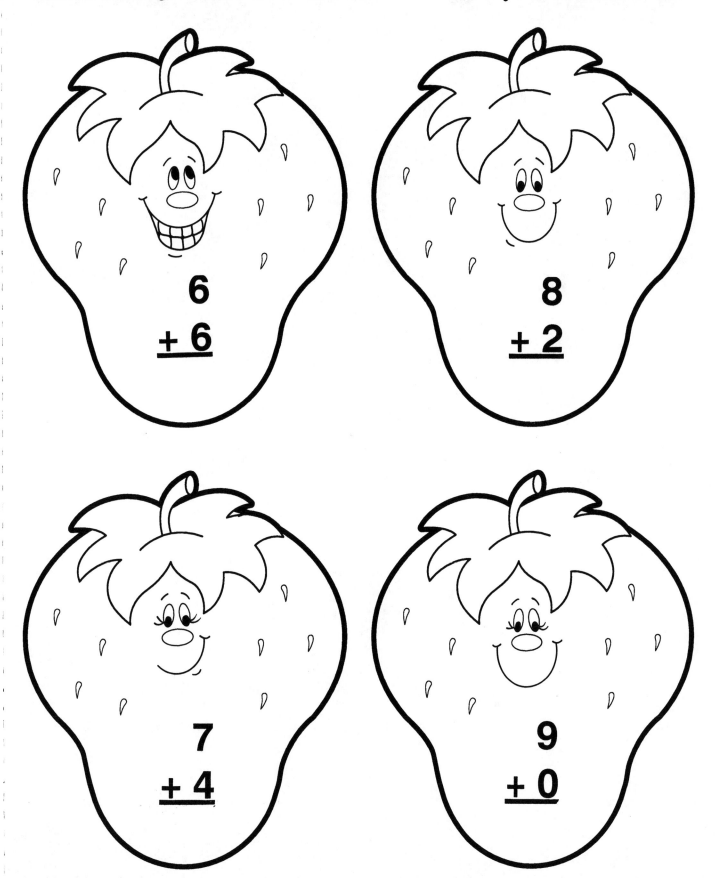

6
+ 6

8
+ 2

7
+ 4

9
+ 0

*Color and cut out small strawberries and mount on tagboard. Laminate and store in plastic pocket or bag.

"Berry" Sweet Numbers

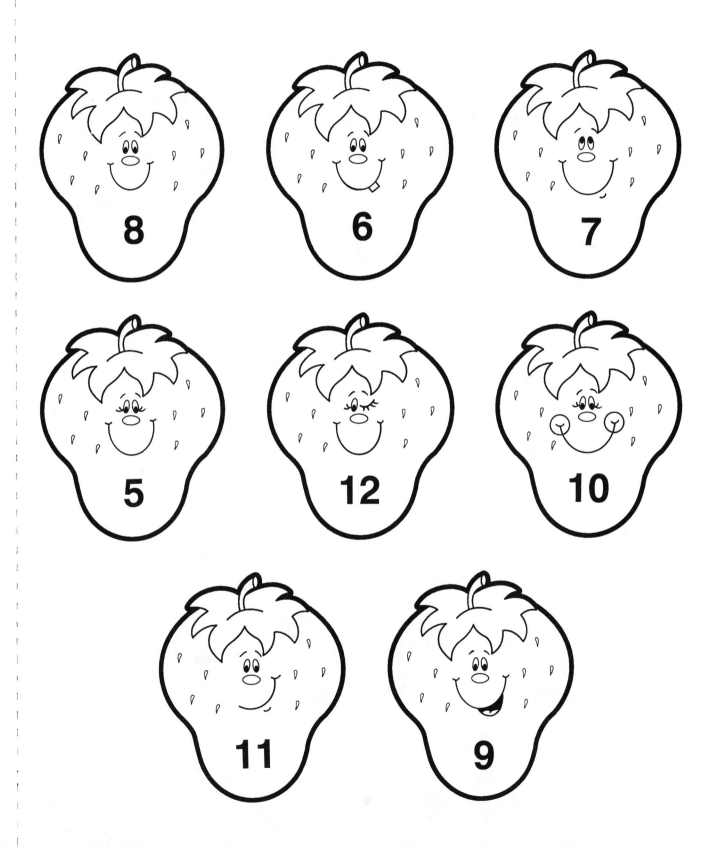

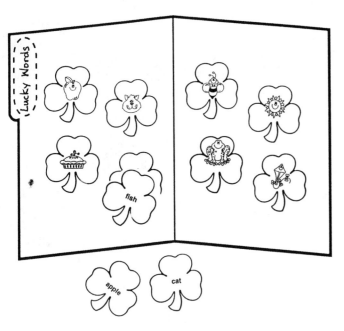

*Mount on file folder tab.

Lucky Words
Matching words and pictures

Game: Lucky Words
Skill: Matching words and pictures
Game Includes: Eight word shamrocks and eight picture shamrocks
How to Make:
1. Color and cut out shamrocks.
2. Mount picture shamrocks in folder and word shamrocks on tagboard.
3. Cut out game label and mount on file folder tab.
4. Color, cut out and mount game title on front of folder.
5. Cut out "How to Play" and mount on outside of folder.
6. For durability, laminate folder and game pieces. Store pieces in plastic pocket or bag.

How to Play: Match each word shamrock to the correct picture shamrock.
---

*Color and cut out game title. Mount on front of folder.

*Color and cut out picture shamrocks and mount in folder.

Lucky Words

245

*Color and cut out picture shamrocks and mount in folder.

Lucky Words

*Color and cut out word shamrocks and mount on tagboard.
Laminate and store word shamrocks in plastic pocket or bag.

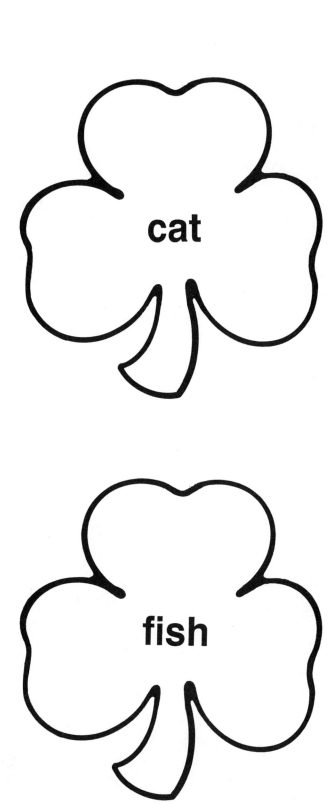

*Color and cut out word shamrocks and mount on tagboard.
Laminate and store word shamrocks in plastic pocket or bag.

Lucky Words

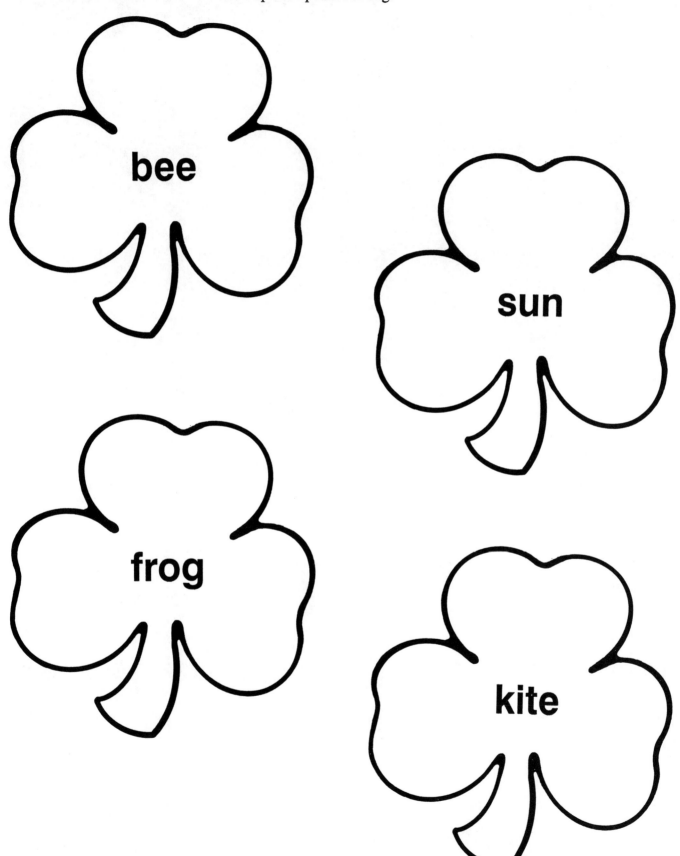

bee

sun

frog

kite

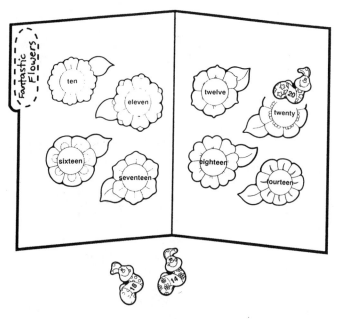

*Mount on file folder tab.

┌─────────────────────────────────┐
│ **Fantastic Flowers**   │
│ **Matching numerals and number words** │
└─────────────────────────────────┘

Game: Fantastic Flowers
Skill: Matching numerals and number words (1-20)
Game Includes: Eight flowers and eight worms
How to Make:
1. Color and cut out flowers and worms.
2. Mount flowers in folder and worms on tagboard.
3. Cut out game label and mount on file folder tab.
4. Color, cut out and mount game title on front of folder.
5. Cut out "How to Play" and mount on outside of folder.
6. For durability, laminate folder and game pieces. Store pieces in plastic pocket or bag.

┌─────────────────────────────────┐
│ **How to Play:** Match each nu- │
│ meral worm to the correct num- │
│ ber word flower.   │
└─────────────────────────────────┘

*Color and cut out game title. Mount on front of folder.

*Color and cut out flowers and mount in folder.

Fantastic Flowers

*Color and cut out flowers and mount in folder.

Fantastic Flowers

Fantastic Flowers

*Mount on file folder tab.

Rain Clouds
Forming compound words

Game: Rain Clouds
Skill: Forming compound words
Game Includes: Eight clouds and eight raindrops
How to Make:
1. Color and cut out clouds and raindrops.
2. Mount clouds in folder and raindrops on tagboard.
3. Cut out game label and mount on file folder tab.
4. Color, cut out and mount game title on front of folder.
5. Cut out "How to Play" and mount on outside of folder.
6. Cut out "Answer Key" and mount on back of folder.
7. For durability, laminate folder and game pieces. Store pieces in plastic pocket or bag.

How to Play: Match each raindrop to the correct cloud to form a compound word.

Answer Key
cupcake
doorbell
grapevine
doghouse
drumstick
seashell
butterfly
football

*Color and cut out game title. Mount on front of folder.

*Color and cut out clouds and mount in folder.

foot

sea

dog

door

WELCOME

*Color and cut out clouds and mount in folder.

butter

cup

grape

drum

*Color and cut out raindrops and mount on tagboard.
Laminate and store raindrops in plastic pocket or bag.

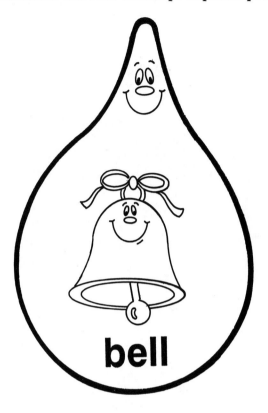

bell

cake

stick

house

*Color and cut out raindrops and mount on tagboard.
Laminate and store raindrops in plastic pocket or bag.

Rain Clouds

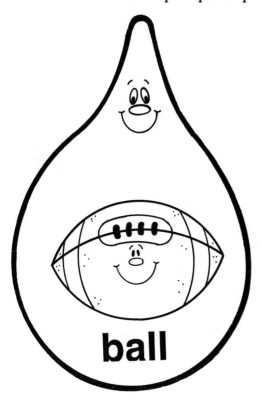

ball

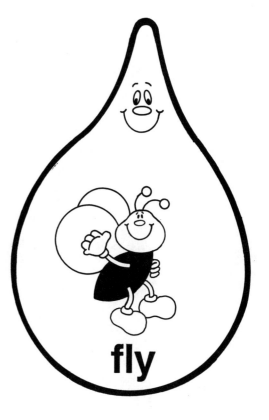

fly

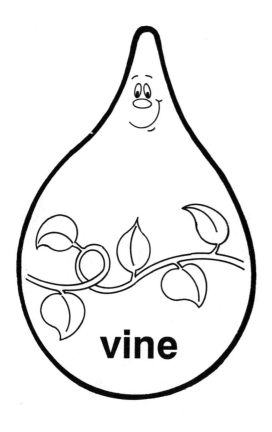

vine

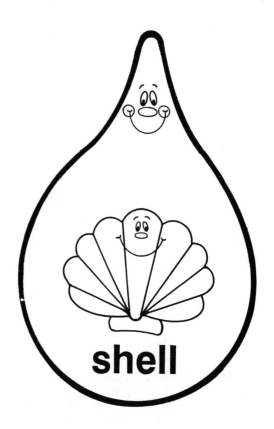

shell

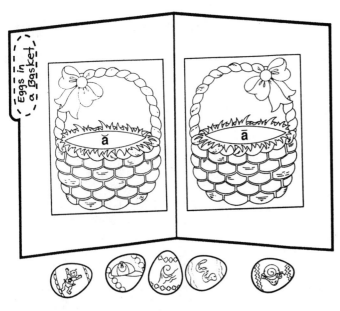

*Mount on file folder tab.

Eggs in a Basket
Identifying long and short "a"

Game: Eggs in a Basket
Skill: Identifying long and short "a"
Game Includes: Two baskets and nine eggs
How to Make:
1. Color and cut out baskets and eggs.
2. Mount baskets in folder and eggs on tagboard.
3. Cut out game label and mount on file folder tab.
4. Color, cut out and mount game title on front of folder.
5. Cut out "How to Play" and mount on outside of folder.
6. For durability, laminate folder and game pieces. Store pieces in plastic pocket or bag.

How to Play: Match the word on each egg to the correct long or short "a" basket.

*Color and cut out game title. Mount on front of folder.

Answer Key	
long a	*short a*
snake	apple
wave	cat
cake	rabbit
baby	cap
snail	

271

*Color and cut out eggs and mount on tagboard.
Laminate and store eggs in plastic pocket or bag.

Eggs in a Basket

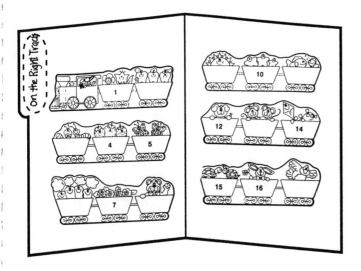

*Mount on file folder tab.

On the Right Track
Sequencing numbers

Game: On the Right Track
Skill: Sequencing numbers
Game Includes: One train engine and seventeen cars
How to Make:
1. Color and cut out train engine and cars.
2. Mount train engine and cars in folder.
3. Cut out game label and mount on file folder tab.
4. Color, cut out and mount game title on front of folder.
5. Cut out "How to Play" and mount on outside of folder.
6. For durability and to make it write-on/wipe-off, laminate folder.

How to Play: Use a grease pencil to fill in missing numbers in sequence to complete the train.

*Color and cut out game title. Mount on front of folder.

*Color and cut out train engine and cars and mount in folder.

On the Right Track

281

*Color and cut out cars and mount in folder.

On the Right Track

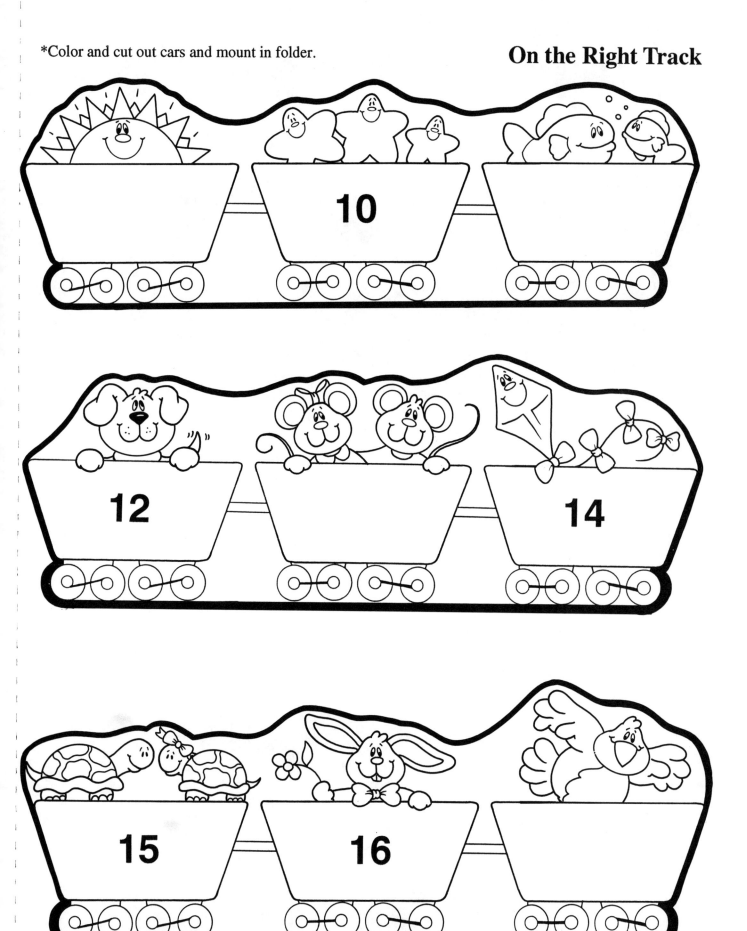

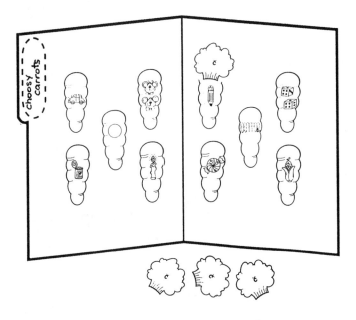

Game: Choosy Carrots

Game: Choosy Carrots
Skill: Identifying hard and soft "c"
Game Includes: Ten carrots and ten carrot tops
How to Make:
1. Color and cut out carrots and carrot tops.
2. Mount carrots in folder and carrot tops on tagboard.
3. Cut out game label and mount on file folder tab.
4. Color, cut out and mount game title on front of folder.
5. Cut out "How to Play" and mount on outside of folder.
6. Cut out "Answer Key" and mount on back of folder.
7. For durability, laminate folder and game pieces. Store pieces in plastic pocket or bag.

*Mount on file folder tab.

Choosy Carrots
Identifying hard and soft "c"

How to Play: Match each carrot top to its correct carrot to identify the hard or soft "c".

*Color and cut out game title. Mount on front of folder.

Answer Key

hard "c"	soft "c"
candy	mice
corn	dice
candle	fence
can	pencil
car	circle

*Color and cut out carrots and mount in folder.

Choosy Carrots

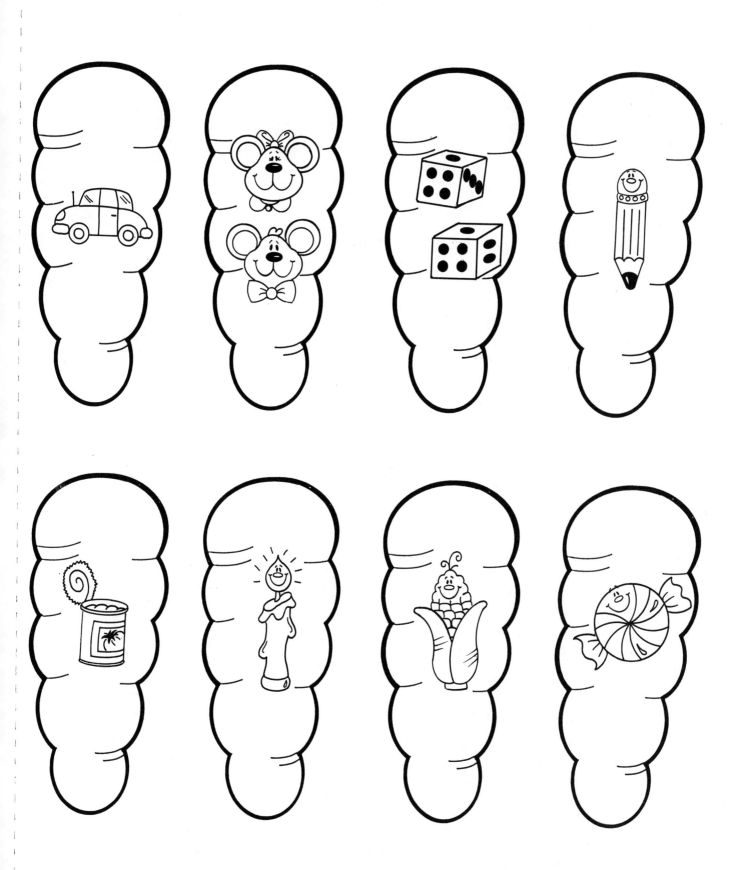

287

*Color and cut out carrots and carrot tops. Mount carrots in folder and carrot tops on tagboard. Laminate and store tops in plastic pocket or bag.

Choosy Carrots

*Color and cut out carrot tops and mount on tagboard. Laminate and store carrot tops in plastic pocket or bag.

Choosy Carrots

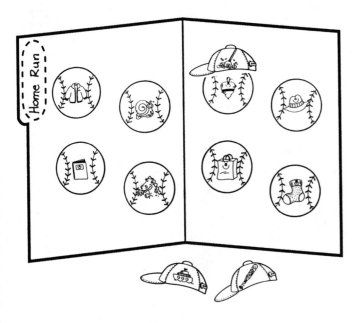

*Mount on file folder tab.

Home Run
Rhyming words

Game: Home Run
Skill: Rhyming words
Game Includes: Eight baseball hats and eight baseballs
How to Make:
1. Color and cut out baseball hats and baseballs.
2. Mount baseballs in folder and baseball hats on tagboard.
3. Cut out game label and mount on file folder tab.
4. Color, cut out and mount game title on front of folder.
5. Cut out "How to Play" and mount on outside of folder.
6. For durability, laminate folder and game pieces. Store pieces in plastic pocket or bag.

How to Play: Match each baseball to its rhyming baseball hat.

*Color and cut out game title. Mount on front of folder.

*Color and cut out baseballs and mount in folder.

Home Run

*Color and cut out baseballs and mount in folder.

Home Run

*Color and cut out baseball hats and mount on tagboard.
Laminate and store hats in plastic pocket or bag.

Home Run

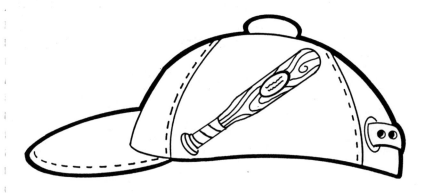

299

*Color and cut out baseball hats and mount on tagboard.
Laminate and store baseball hats in plastic pocket or bag.

Home Run

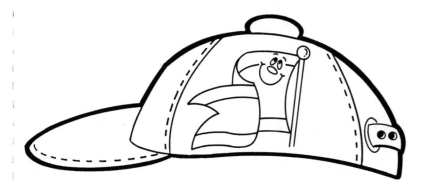

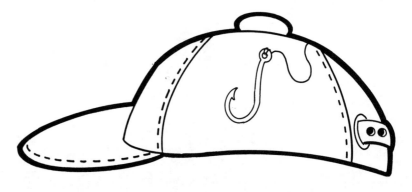

301

*Mount on file folder tab.

Game: Circus Addition

Skill: Adding (1-15)

Game Includes: Eight elephants, eight peanuts and answer key

How to Make:

1. Color and cut out elephants and peanuts.
2. Mount elephants in folder and peanuts on tagboard.
3. Cut out game label and mount on file folder tab.
4. Color, cut out and mount game title on front of folder.
5. Cut out "How to Play" and mount on outside of folder.
6. Cut out "Answer Key" and mount on back of folder.
7. For durability, laminate folder and game pieces. Store pieces in plastic pocket or bag.

How to Play: Solve each problem by placing the correct peanut next to the elephant.

Answer Key

$7 + 5 = 12$

$8 + 6 = 14$

$4 + 5 = 9$

$4 + 9 = 13$

$3 + 8 = 11$

$10 + 5 = 15$

$5 + 2 = 7$

$6 + 4 = 10$

*Color and cut out game title. Mount on front of folder.

*Color and cut out elephants and mount in folder.

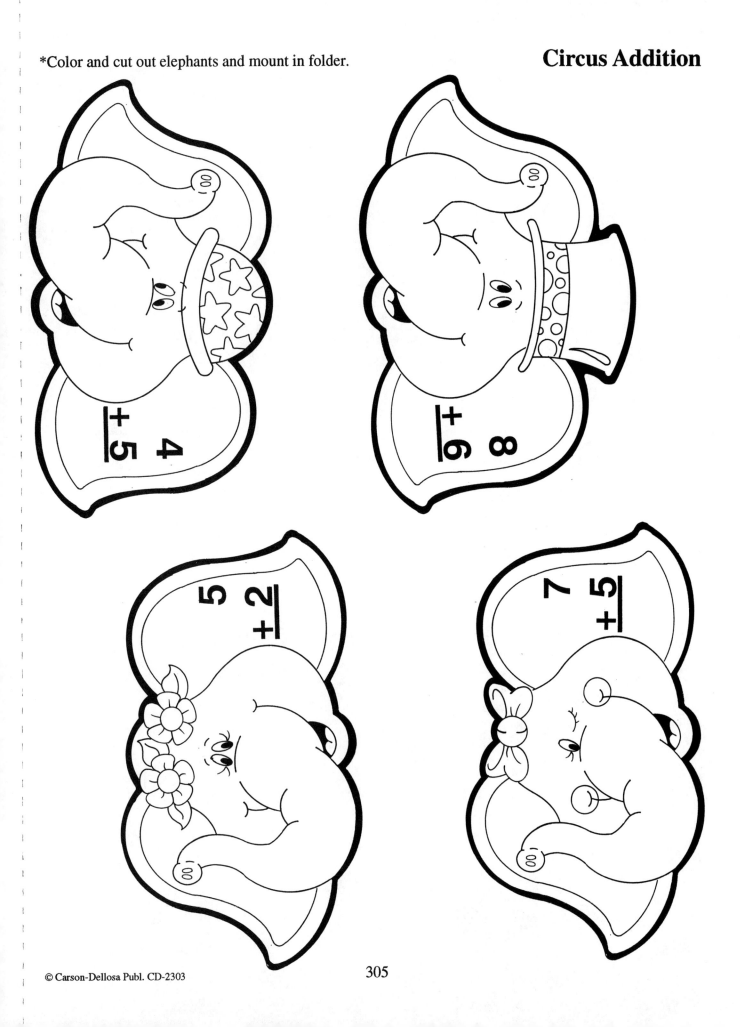

$$4 + 5$$

$$8 + 6$$

$$5 + 2$$

$$7 + 5$$

*Color and cut out elephants and mount in folder.

Circus Addition

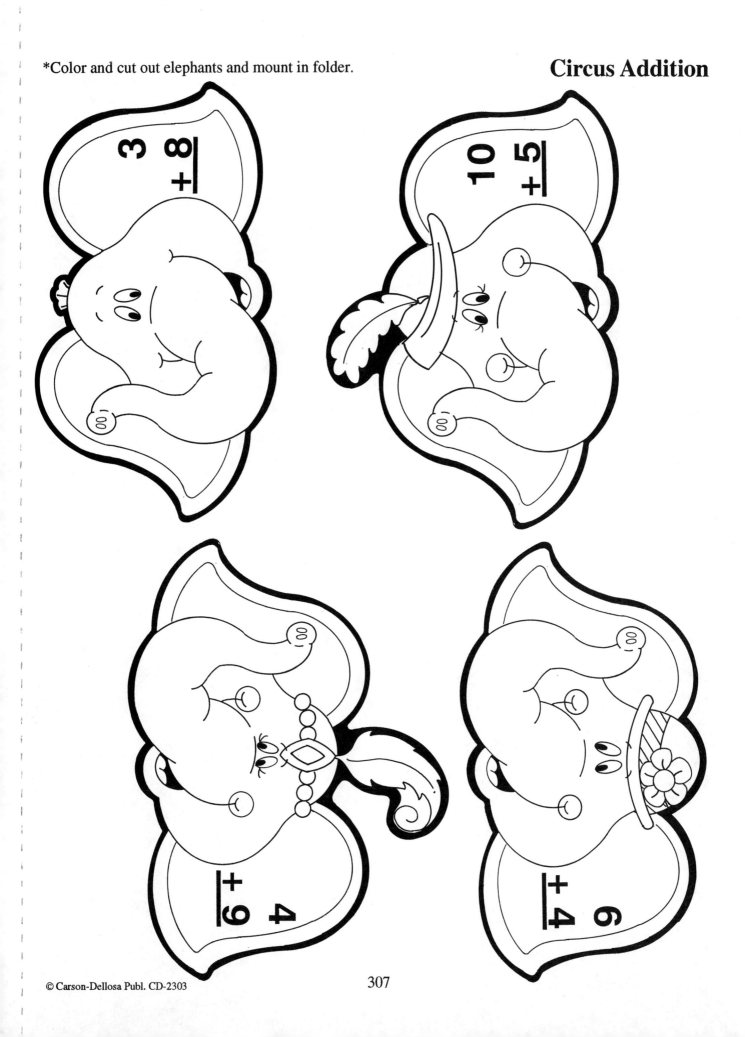

*Color and cut out peanuts and mount on tagboard.
Laminate and store peanuts in plastic pocket or bag.

Circus Addition

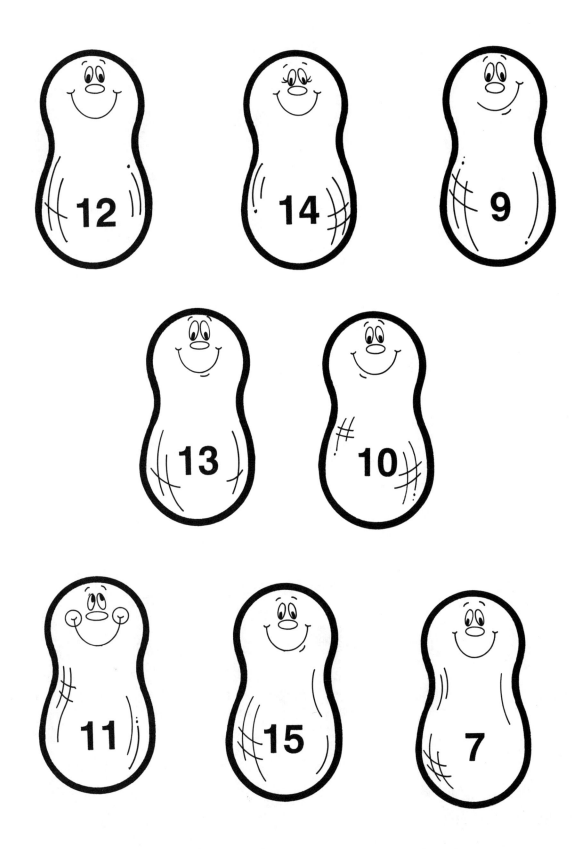

*Mount on file folder tab.

The Big Cheese
Subtracting (1-12)

Game: The Big Cheese
Skill: Subtracting (1-12)
Game Includes: Eight mice, eight pieces of cheese and answer key
How to Make:
1. Color and cut out mice and cheese.
2. Mount cheese in folder and mice on tagboard.
3. Cut out game label and mount on file folder tab.
4. Color, cut out, and mount game title on front of folder.
5. Cut out "How to Play" and mount on outside of folder.
6. Cut out "Answer Key" and mount on back of folder.
7. For durability, laminate folder and game pieces. Store pieces in plastic pocket or bag.

How to Play: Solve the problem on each piece of cheese by placing the correct mouse next to it.

Answer Key
12 - 4 = 8
9 - 3 = 6
11 - 2 = 9
7 - 4 = 3
10 - 3 = 7
6 - 2 = 4
8 - 6 = 2
5 - 0 = 5

311

*Color and cut out game title. Mount on front of folder.

*Color and cut out cheese and mount in folder.

The Big Cheese

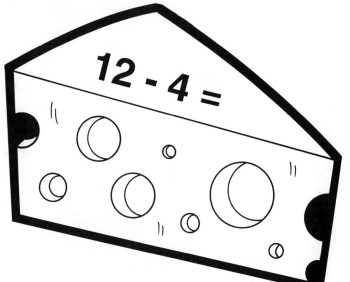

12 - 4 =

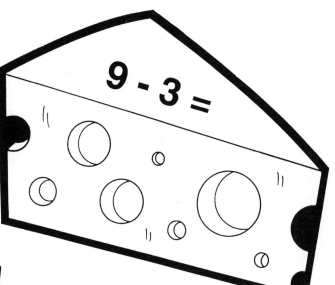

9 - 3 =

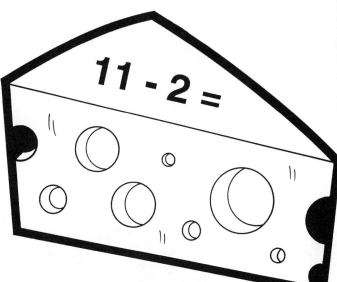

11 - 2 =

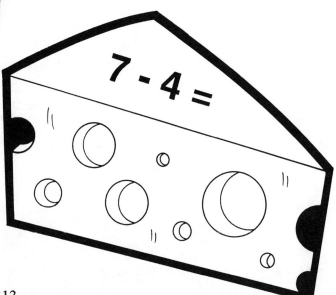

7 - 4 =

*Color and cut out cheese and mount in folder.

The Big Cheese

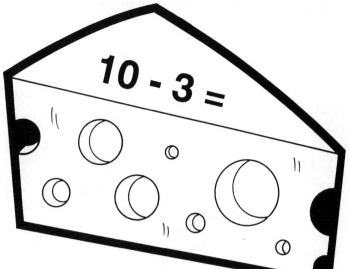

10 - 3 =

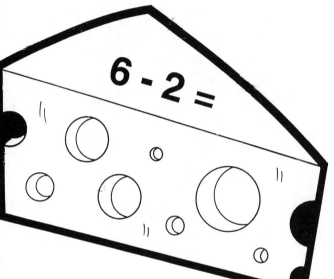

6 - 2 =

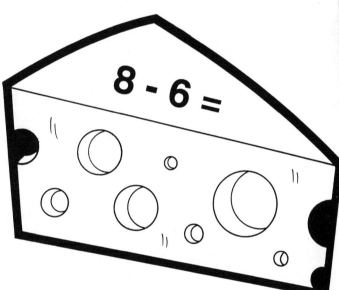

8 - 6 =

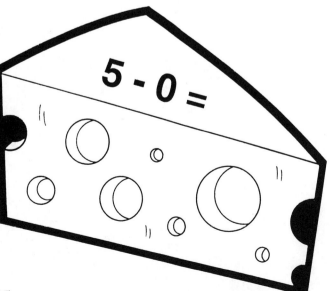

5 - 0 =

*Color and cut out mice and mount on tagboard.
Laminate and store mice in plastic pocket or bag.

The Big Cheese

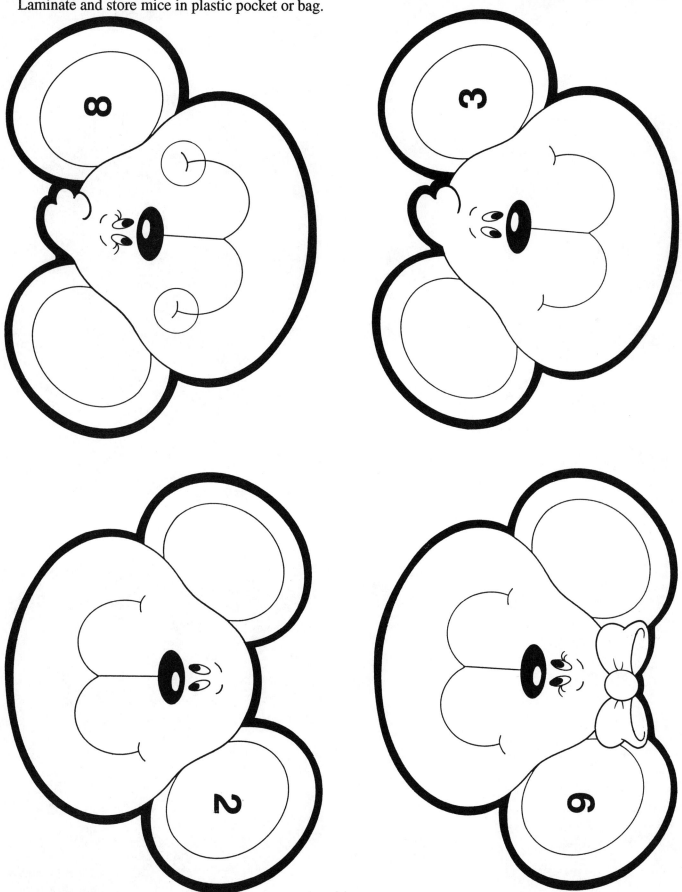

The Big Cheese

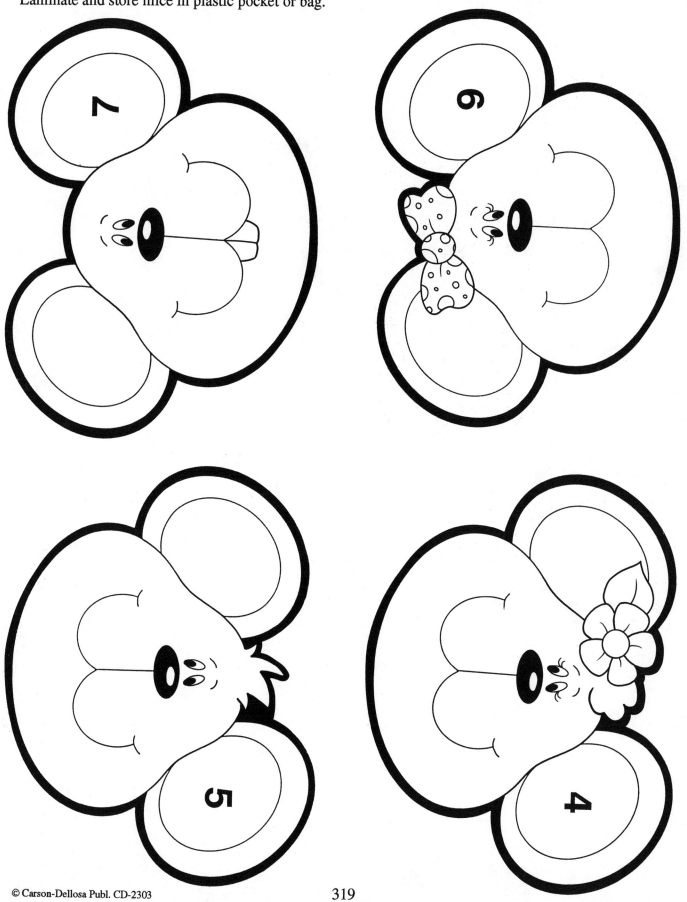

319

*Mount on file folder tab.

Cruisin' for Numbers
Identifying "one less" in number sequences

Game: Cruisin' for Numbers

Skill: Identifying "one less" in number sequences

Game Includes: Eight cars and 16 wheels

How to Make:

1. Color and cut out cars and wheels.
2. Mount cars in folder and wheels on tagboard.
3. Cut out game label and mount on file folder tab.
4. Color, cut out and mount game title on front of folder.
5. Cut out "How to Play" and mount on outside of folder.
6. For durability, laminate folder and game pieces. Store pieces in plastic pocket or bag.

How to Play: Match two wheels to each car to show the "one less" number sequence.

*Color and cut out game title. Mount on front of folder.

321

*Color and cut out cars and mount in folder.

Cruisin' for Numbers

Cruisin' for Numbers

*Color and cut out wheels and mount on tagboard.
Laminate and store wheels in plastic pocket or bag.

3   7   12   9

4   8   9   2

6   11   10   3

7   5   4   8

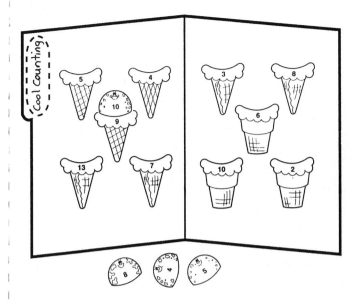

Cool Counting
Adding "one more" number

Game: Cool Counting

Skill: Adding "one more" number

Game Includes: Ten ice cream cones and ten ice cream scoops

How to Make:

1. Color and cut out ice cream cones and ice cream scoops.
2. Mount ice cream cones in folder and ice cream scoops on tagboard.
3. Cut out game label and mount on file folder tab.
4. Color, cut out and mount game title on front of folder.
5. Cut out "How to Play" and mount on outside of folder.
6. For durability, laminate folder and game pieces. Store pieces in plastic pocket or bag.

How to Play: Match each ice cream scoop to the correct ice cream cone to add "one more."

*Color and cut out game title. Mount on front of folder.

COOL COUNTING

*Color and cut out ice cream cones and mount in folder.

Cool Counting

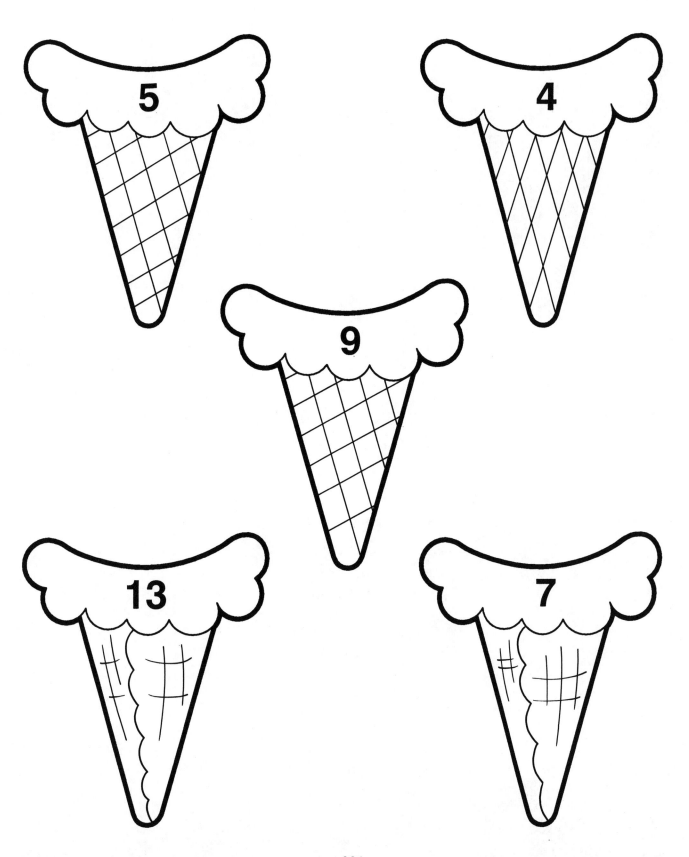

*Color and cut out ice cream cones and mount in folder.

Cool Counting

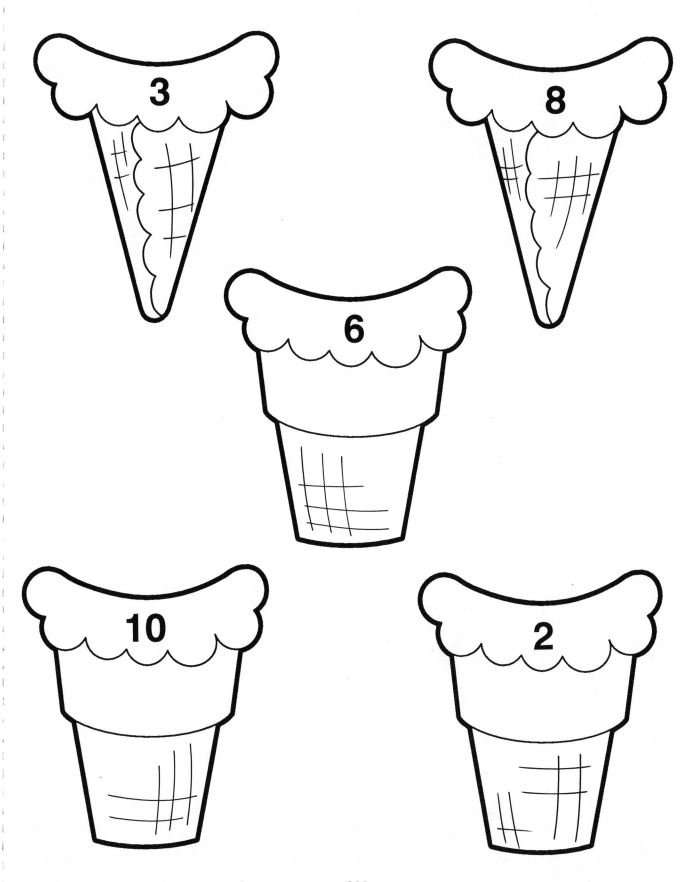

*Color and cut out ice cream scoops and mount on tagboard.
Laminate and store ice cream scoops in plastic pocket or bag.

Cool Counting

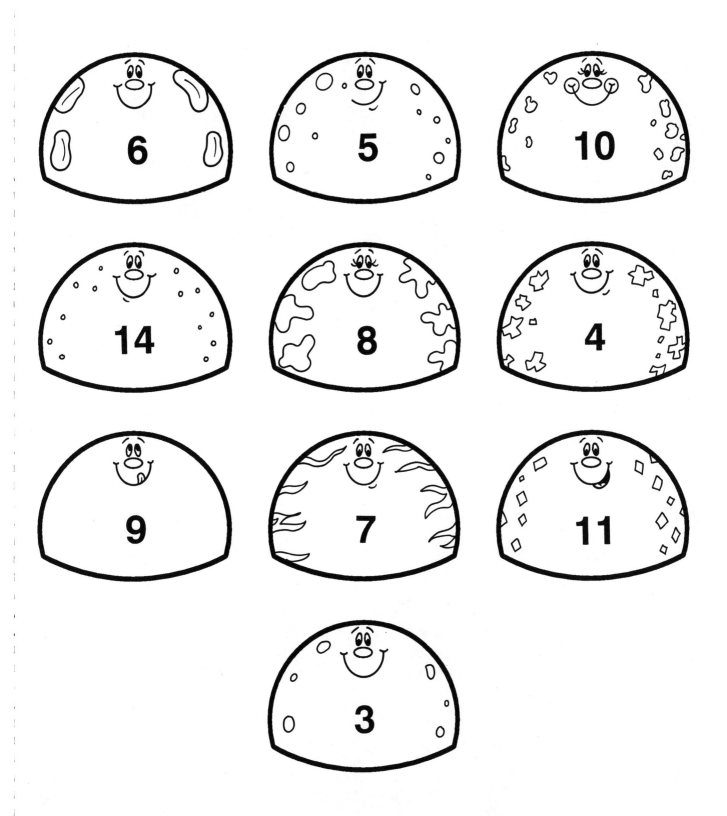

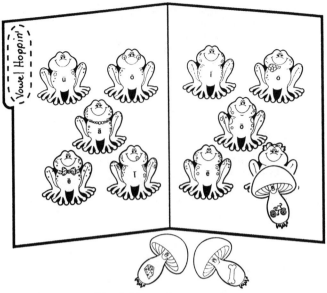

*Mount on file folder tab.

> ## Vowel Hoppin'
> **Reviewing long vowels**

Game: Vowel Hoppin'
Skill: Reviewing long vowels
Game Includes: Ten toads and ten toadstools
How to Make:

1. Color and cut out toads and toadstools.
2. Mount toads in folder and toadstools on tagboard.
3. Cut out game label and mount on file folder tab.
4. Color, cut out and mount game title on front of folder.
5. Cut out "How to Play" and mount on outside of folder.
6. For durability, laminate folder and game pieces. Store pieces in plastic pocket or bag.

> **How to Play:** Match each toadstool to the correct toad to show the long vowel sound.

*Color and cut out game title. Mount on front of folder.

*Color and cut out toads and mount in folder.

*Color and cut out toads and mount in folder.

Vowel Hoppin'

*Color and cut out toadstools and mount on tagboard.
Laminate and store toadstools in plastic pocket or bag.

Vowel Hoppin'

*Color and cut out toadstools and mount on tagboard.
Laminate and store toadstools in plastic pocket or bag.

Vowel Hoppin'

Ladybug, Ladybug
Learning number words (1-14)

Game: Ladybug, Ladybug
Skill: Learning number words (1-14)
Game Includes: Eight ladybugs and eight ladybug shells
How to Make:
1. Color and cut out ladybugs and ladybug shells.
2. Mount ladybugs in folder and ladybug shells on tagboard.
3. Cut out game label and mount on file folder tab.
4. Color, cut out and mount game title on front of folder.
5. Cut out "How to Play" and mount on outside of folder.
6. For durability, laminate folder and game pieces. Store pieces in plastic pocket or bag.

How to Play: Count sets on ladybug and then place the correct number word shell on the ladybug's back.

*Color and cut out game title. Mount on front of folder.

*Color and cut out ladybugs and shells. Mount ladybugs in folder. Mount shells on tagboard. Laminate and store in plastic pocket or bag.

Ladybug, Ladybug

seven

ten

six

eleven

*Color and cut out ladybugs and shells. Mount ladybugs in folder.
Mount shells on tagboard. Laminate and store shells in plastic pocket or bag.

Ladybug, Ladybug

five

thirteen

eight

fourteen

351